Weeds in the Garden

The Growing Danger of Fraud Taking Root in the Church

Verne Hargrave, CPA, CFE

NACBA
PRESS

ISBN: 0-9705433-9-5

©2009

NACBA Press is the publishing arm of the National Association of Church Business Administration.

100 N. Central Expy. • Suite 914

Richardson, Texas 75080-5326

(800) 898-8085 • (972) 699-7555

(972) 699-7617 Fax

www.nacba.net

Acknowledgments

My thanks go to many people who have helped me in this journey. First, Dr. Judy Stamey not only provided much needed editing and encouragement, but also conceived the idea for this book.

I am also grateful to our friends at the National Association of Church Business Administration: Phill Martin, Simeon May and Rose Ella McCleary who enthusiastically helped me along the way.

Special thanks go to my colleagues at PSK, particularly my partners who have extended me the freedom to pursue projects such as this. Also, I am appreciative to Ann Denton and Tnai Mason who I repeatedly interrupted from their busy routines to serve as my "sounding boards."

Finally, I am thankful for my wife, who has been a constant source of encouragement, not simply during the writing of this book, but ever since we first held hands in the halls of Arlington High School.

Table of Contents

Preface

A frequent weather pattern where I live, in North Central Texas, is the "cool front." Most of the time cool fronts are very welcome events because they bring relief from the oppressive heat that often blankets our region. At other times, cool winds sweep down from the Rockies and collide with warm, moist air from the Gulf of Mexico. The result of this collision is why our region is part of what has been aptly named, "Tornado Alley." When this type of pattern takes place, the severe storm warnings go into effect and everyone, from first responders to civilians, takes precautionary measures.

However, when the front is still far off on the horizon, the weather pattern can actually be quite beautiful. Mammoth cloud formations form, stretching thousands of miles into the sky. The sun's rays strike the clouds creating a range of colors from white, yellow, orange, pink and black. (However, if you see green, it may be time to take cover!) At night, the lightening shows can be spectacular. I have spent many hours standing mesmerized by the incredible beauty.

Occasionally, the reverie will be interrupted by the sound of thunder rumbling across the prairies. This sound, sometimes resembling muffled drums, announces that although the sight is pretty, trouble is on its way.

A parallel can be drawn with the contemporary church in America. In spite of the recent economic downturn, new churches continue to be planted. Buildings are being constructed and equipped with the latest high-tech gadgets to create effective worship experiences. New and exciting ways are being used to expand outreach to an increasingly secular culture. Looking from afar, things look good. But, if you listen closely, thunder can be heard rumbling across the landscape announcing that all may not be right.

One of these thunder claps is fraud: economic misbehavior in the church house. It seems that there is not one week that goes by without hearing of another church or ministry being taken advantage of, or participating in fraudulent behavior.

I have spent the better part of my career in public accounting providing consulting services to churches and ministries. I have seen quite a few "storms" pass through the church environment and have had to counsel, cry with, and help quite a few congregations through some extremely difficult situations. As a result, I have become used to this side of church life and am under no illusion that everything is hunky-dory in the church world.

But, recent events have begun to worry me; someone who used to think he had pretty much seen it all. In my opinion, occupational fraud just may be the newest serious threat to the church.

Since the collapse of Enron, most auditors have been routinely recommending that their clients implement stronger fraud prevention measures beginning by performing a fraud risk assessment. But, for the most part, this is not taking place in the church environment. Most business administrators are stretched for time as it is and cannot squeeze one more thing into their tightly packed schedules. Also, because the task is so immense, and the ways a church can be abused are so varied, most business administrators would not even know where to begin, even if they had the time; fraud protection is complicated.

Preface

The purpose of this short book is to help break this logjam created by these very common reasons for not taking anti-fraud steps. As you make your way through its pages, please keep three things in mind. First, it was my intention to keep the book short. Creating a huge manual might scare off time-starved administrators. Second, the book can be the starting point of a church's fraud prevention measures; the basis on which to perform a fraud risk assessment. Third, it is organized in such a way as to take some of the complications out of the process. After two chapters which define and describe fraud, come ten chapters, each represented by a question every church should ask of itself. Each question represents an important aspect in fraud prevention.

It is my prayer that this book can serve as a guide to help your church get prepared for the storms which are sure to sweep over the prairie.[1]

---

[1] A note needs to be added concerning the case studies presented at the end of many of the chapters. With the exception of those presented in my concluding remarks, these case studies have been "sanitized." While the events are real and were drawn from actual fraud occurrences, the names of churches, individuals and cities are fictional. My goal is to help the reader understand how these things can happen, not pile on unfortunate churches that have gone through the fire of fraud victimization.

Weeds in the Garden

Jesus told them another parable: "The kingdom of heaven is like a man who sowed good seed in his field. But while everyone was sleeping, his enemy came and sowed weeds among the wheat, and went away. When the wheat sprouted and formed heads, then the weeds also appeared...

Matthew 13:24-26, New International Version

"For crying out loud, we are a church!"
"We trust our people!"
"Doing this is the same as calling our people crooks!"
These are some of the worn out objections I get when I suggest that a church should take fraud prevention measures. Translated, what they are telling me is this: "It could *never* happen here."

There could be nothing further from the truth.
The Bible stands alone in bringing truth to light in *all* aspects of life, including church finances. Christ's parable, often called the *"Parable of the Wheat and the Tares,"* reinforces the fact that churches can be targets of fraud just as easily as businesses. This passage also illustrates another fact about financial misbehavior in the church: many fraud attacks are "inside" jobs perpetrated by individuals placed in positions of trust. Often, these people are just like the weeds in the parable, appearing to be one thing while being something altogether different.

Unfortunately, when it comes to church finances, this parable is played out in the church all too frequently. Entering "church embezzlement" on an Internet search engine will return a seemingly endless stream of examples of individuals with financial responsibilities who have violated the trust of the churches they serve. More frightening is the fact that the evidence of this is not limited to anecdotal stories. Statistics are beginning to reflect a startling truth: there are weeds in the garden. For example, the Association of Certified Fraud Examiners (ACFE) in their *2008 Report to the Nation on Occupational Fraud and Abuse*, states that 14.6% of reported fraud incidents occurred in nonprofit organizations with the median loss being $109,000. Churches, by far, make up the largest group of nonprofit organizations in the nation.

Churches are at risk because...

Churches have something crooks want: MONEY! Most church business administrators, who sweat bullets every month over whether or not they will make their budget, might disagree with this but the truth is churches are a *lucrative target*. Other than property and equipment, most churches only have one significant asset, and that is cash. Cash can be found in petty cash boxes, at fund raising volunteers' homes, in safes whose combinations are known by far too many people, and in bank accounts. Also, churches that are in the midst of a building campaign or have a great deal of restricted giving will often have large amounts of idle cash sitting in savings and money market accounts. Needless to say, churches provide a "target-rich" environment for aspiring embezzlers. This brings to mind the quote of a famous bank robber in the thirties who, when asked why he robbed banks, gave a very profound answer: "That's where the money is." This is true for churches, too!

The environment and philosophy of most churches make them attractive targets. Because churches are in the "redemption" business, they often find it difficult to implement strong business controls. Part of the problem is that churches tend to operate under a *"trust and forgive"* attitude rather than *"trust, but verify."* Many church leaders have a hard time even admitting that such a thing could happen in their midst. Bad things do indeed happen to good churches. Read the scripture: *"He did not say this because he cared about the poor but because he was a thief; as keeper of the money bag, he used to help himself to what was put into it." (John 12:6, NIV)* The "he" John was referring to was Judas, one of Christ's twelve disciples. This ought to be proof to anyone in a position of church financial leadership that *it can happen anywhere!*

The management style and structure of many churches invites bad behavior. Many churches do not take the time to develop well defined operating and control practices and procedures. As a result there are no clearly established guidelines for conducting financial transactions, especially in regard to the handling of cash receipts and disbursements. This environment is the perfect smoke screen for illicit behavior. Even an auditor finds it very difficult to tell the difference between messy accounting and financial misdeeds. Exacerbating these situations are the ever-present budget constraints of most churches which result in the inability to hire a sufficient number of employees to insure an adequate separation of duties. This can result in too many of the tasks becoming the responsibility of one individual. If this person is of high integrity the church may never have a problem; however, if a person of lesser character is ever placed in the position…

The Church is the largest volunteer organization in the world. Since its inception, volunteers have been the backbone of the church. Most of the original apostles were "tent making" evangelists, named for the Apostle Paul who funded his life and ministry by this profession. Today, in spite of the increasing reliance of congregations on paid staff, the church could not survive without the volunteers who feed the hungry, visit the sick, teach Sunday School classes, and perform countless acts of service to their church. Volunteerism also extends to the financial tasks of the church with many volunteers serving on finance committees, passing offering plates, counting and recording tithes and offerings, and transporting offerings to the bank. While a church could not live without volunteers, it should be aware of certain challenges that the use of volunteers can present. For example, volunteers seldom receive formal training and have limited financial backgrounds which can result in a naïveté in financial matters. This can make such people "easy marks" for unscrupulous embezzlers. Also, in some churches volunteers tend to consist of friends and relatives, thereby resulting in a lack of independence and objectivity increasing the possibilities for collusion. Finally, scheduled turnover of board and committee members and frequent resignations by board members due to time constraints can lead to inconsistency in financial transaction processes, creating another situation in which fraudsters thrive.

No one is looking. The vast majority of churches and ministries in the United States have no outside audit, review, or consulting. If an organization never opens its books or its practices to outside, independent eyes, it is putting itself in a high state of risk. By doing so, however, the church adds a layer of protection around its assets, staff, and volunteers and stays abreast of the latest trends affecting the church environment. This form of accountability serves notice to both the church membership and those who want to abuse the church that financial matters of the church are taken seriously and closely guarded, but open to scrutiny. This practice alone may be enough to keep the wolves out of the hen house.

There is poor tone at the top. The mood is set at the top of any organization, and this is especially true in the church. If financial matters are not important at the senior levels, it is certain they will not be important at the lower levels, either. This often results in a casual atmosphere concerning accountability and stewardship from top to bottom. Needless to say, persons given to fraud love these situations.

How does it happen?

Churches that decide to be proactive about fraud prevention begin by performing some form of fraud assessment to determine where their "soft spots" may be. Unfortunately, many church fraud risk assessments are too narrow because they tend to focus exclusively on the Sunday offering procedures. On one hand this is good, because tithes and offerings are the lifeblood of the financial activity of the church (You have to have offerings before you can spend a budget!), but this is not where most of their effort needs to go.

There are two good reasons why churches need to expand their fraud prevention efforts far beyond tithes and offerings, count teams, money bags, and the like. First, most churches already do a pretty good job of monitoring tithes and offerings. Auditors rarely find a church that has not ratcheted down the offering processes with locking money bags, dual access safes, rotating teller teams, and even armored cars in some cases. While not letting their guard down in this area, churches should expand their fraud assessment and prevention steps to other areas to determine if any points of weakness can be found.

There is another reason for churches to expand their fraud assessments past the Sunday offerings. More frauds seem to take place in the cash *"outflow"* processes than in the cash *"inflow"* processes. Outflow refers primarily to the accounts payable and payroll functions of the church. The ACFE Report to the Nation presented statistics showing the types of frauds perpetrated on nonprofits. Interestingly, skimming and cash larceny, (which in a church environment generally would take place during the Sunday offering process) trailed behind other cash outflows types of fraud.

The most frequent types of frauds were:

- **Corruption** – *Examples include bribes and kickbacks given to purchasers. An individual with purchasing and/or bill paying approval responsibilities may make excessive or inappropriate purchases in order to obtain favors from vendors.*

- **False expense reimbursements and credit card abuse** – *This type of fraud makes the news quite frequently and is of extreme interest to the IRS due to excess benefit and private inurement issues.*

- **Check tampering** - *Lack of segregation of accounting duties can lead to check falsifications through forgeries and other alterations. This is the most common type of fraudulent behavior in smaller organizations. Churches need to understand that dual signature requirements, by themselves, are little or no protection against embezzlers bold enough to forge.*

- **Payroll fraud** – *Fictitious time cards and phantom employees are the most common examples of this abuse. Fraudsters find payroll an appealing target because labor costs are usually the single largest operating cost of a church and their misbehavior is much easier to hide among the larger numbers.*

Could we be on the wrong track?

Churches and other ministries are doing things about it; however, by referring once again to ACFE statistics, it appears they may be doing the wrong things. According to the *2008 Report to the Nation*, over half of the fraud incidents in the survey were initially detected either by *anonymous tips* or by *accident*. Strong internal controls caught another twenty-five percent of the incidents in the study. Interestingly, frauds detected by external audits amounted to less than fifteen percent of the total. In defense of my profession, this statistic reinforces a point auditors make in engagement and audit committee letters. While auditors do consider fraud risk and conduct certain tests to detect fraud, they do not look at all transactions. Accordingly, unqualified or "clean" opinions can be issued even though fraudulent activities might have occurred and gone undetected. In spite of the fact that auditors' fraud risk assessment steps have been enhanced in recent years, the primary focus of a certified audit remains the expression of an opinion on whether or not a set of financial statements is presented in accordance with generally accepted accounting principles.

When these facts combine with what churches and nonprofits are doing to prevent fraud, a disturbing thing emerges. Based on the ACFE reports, the overwhelming fraud prevention measure being employed by nonprofits and churches is the external audit. What this reveals is that churches and ministries are spending most of their fraud prevention money on measures that have had less success in detecting fraud than other, less expensive methods.

What can be done about it?

To begin with, please do not fire your auditor! Audits are important and serve other needs in addition to fraud control. Instead, churches should consider adding measures that have a high degree of effectiveness in the prevention of fraud. Here are two examples.

First, the most staggering ACFE statistic is that over half of the initial fraud detection was due to *anonymous tips* or by *accident.* Ministries might consider taking advantage of this by implementing an anonymous hotline (accessed by telephone or Web site) in which employees or volunteers can express their concerns without fear of retribution. It cannot be denied that this will be distasteful to many in the church environment, but it is a reflection of the times in which we live. Over the last generation, churches have had to add many "distasteful" chores to their task lists because of the general decline in ethics of our culture. Anyone who has been in the church administration business long will probably recall the initial backlash against background checks. Financial matters are no different and this form of accountability and transparency is becoming much more of a necessity.

Second, according to the ACFE statistics, the most effective fraud prevention technique other than tips and by accident is a strong internal control system. Each church should do what their auditors have probably been recommending in their management letters for the past several years: perform a comprehensive fraud risk assessment. They should take whatever time is necessary and perform a *thorough study* of their processes from a fraud prevention perspective.

For example, here are a few very general steps a church could take:

- *Create ownership in the fraud prevention process by establishing a formal fraud awareness and prevention* **team**.

- *Hold a few initial* **"brain storming"** *sessions to identify potential fraud risks within the church structure and processes.*

- *Perform a* **detailed review** *of church policies, procedures and organizational structure looking particularly for "weak spots" that could be compromised. (Poor separation of duties usually is the main focus of this process.)*

- *Make policy and or procedure* **modifications** *to close down any weaknesses discovered.*

- *Create and implement methods to* **monitor** *the processes in the future.*

This is definitely not a comprehensive list and each church will have to develop a fraud risk assessment plan that works best in its own specific place of ministry, but beginning the process by doing some of these things, a church's eyes can be opened to the dangers it faces and the "weeds" that may be growing in its garden.

Chapter 2

First, Be Sure You Know What You Are Looking For

"Suppose one of you wants to build a tower. Will he not first sit down and estimate the cost to see if he has enough money to complete it?

Luke 14:28, New International Version

During the American Civil War, the Battle of Gettysburg was fought over a three day period, July 1 through July 3, 1864. Two reasons are given why some consider Gettysburg to be the most significant battle of the war. First, more casualties were suffered during this three-day battle than any other Civil War engagement, although the single day casualty mark was set at the Battle of Antietam. But, more importantly, Gettysburg is generally considered the turning point of the war. At Gettysburg, for the first time, the Union army had defeated an army led by General Robert E. Lee. The Confederates were forced to fall back into Virginia, never to attack the North for the duration of the war. This battle, with implications still felt today, culminated in a bloody and tragic event commonly referred to as "Pickett's Charge."

Several years ago, while on vacation, I visited the site of the Battle of Gettysburg. The battle site is extensive, spreading completely over and around the town of Gettysburg, Pennsylvania. Because of this size, it can be a challenge for a visitor to gain a sense of what happened during those three fateful days. The National Park Service, who administers the battleground site, solved this problem by providing trained, certified guides to escort visitors and describe the events. On the advice of a friend I hired one of the guides.

After visiting several of the best known sites; Seminary Ridge, Cemetery Hill, Little Round Top, and Devil's Den, our guide brought us to the site of Pickett's Charge. At this point we got out of the car and stood by a long battery of cannons as the guide told an interesting story. The day of Pickett's Charge, July 3, 1864 was hot, humid and most significant, windless. Prior to the charge, General Lee ordered a horrific artillery bombardment of the Union forces in hopes of knocking out artillery and softening the Union lines. Unfortunately for the Confederates, due to the lack of wind, cannon smoke hovered over the battlefield, obscuring their view of the effectiveness of the barrage. As a result, they could not see what the Union knew: the Confederate Army's aim was terrible. Their shells were coming nowhere close and most were sailing completely over the Union lines. In a shrewd maneuver, the Union artillery commanders silenced their batteries, one by one, to give the appearance to the South that they had been knocked out.

Shortly after, the command was given and Pickett's Charge began. A line of more than twelve thousand soldiers stretching over a mile in length advanced into the smoke. They were expecting to face a softened enemy with little will remaining to fight. Instead, they walked into a death trap because of the unplanned smokescreen. Thousands were killed and wounded and any hopes of winning the war were ended.

What in the world does this have to do with fraud?

It may seem a stretch to compare fraudulent behavior in a church with the sacrifices of the Gettysburg battlefield. Even so, a very significant lesson can be learned and hopefully, applied. Before charging off into the smoke, it would be wise for a church administrator to first be sure he knows exactly what to look for. Once this has been accomplished, fraud, if any, can be handled appropriately. Although it is unlikely that any blood will be spilled if an attempt to confront fraud in a church is bungled, the health of something does rest in the balance. If a fraud assessment is not handled properly, the health of a church may be at considerable risk!

That is why it is important that the first thing an administrator needs to do is make sure he or she knows what it is they are looking for. In other words, a clear understanding must be gained of what financial fraud is before coming up with a battle plan to confront it.

The Association of Certified Fraud Examiners (ACFE) defines occupational fraud as *"the use of one's occupation for personal enrichment through the deliberate misuse or misapplication of the employing organization's resources or assets."*[1] Because of the heavy reliance of churches on volunteers, this definition should be expanded to include unpaid staff in addition to employees. According to the ACFE, there are three major types of occupational fraud; fraudulent financial reporting, corruption and the misappropriation of assets.

---

[1]Association of Certified Fraud Examiners; *Fraud Examiners Manual, 2006, 1.301.*

So, what's cooking...?

Financial statement fraud or, "cooking the books," occurs when the financial condition of an organization is intentionally misrepresented. This can occur when certain elements in financial statements are "cooked" with deliberate *misrepresentations* or important information is *omitted*. The goal is the same in both cases: to deceive the reader of the financial statements.

The formula followed for financial statement fraud normally follows a simple principle: *overstate* income and/or assets or *understate* expenses and/or liabilities. Common methods used are the reporting of fictitious revenues; timing expenses to fit within the most favorable reporting period; inflating asset values and hiding expenses, liabilities and restrictions. The popular assumption is that this is the type of fraud that only the big boys play and involves sophisticated Wall Street operatives and billion dollar corporations.

That is a naïve assumption because, although not as frequent as the other two types of fraud, financial *misreporting* does take place in the religious world.

Here are a few examples:

> • *A church presenting financial statements to a bank in hopes of obtaining a loan, may be tempted to report all of its revenues as unrestricted support, knowing full well that a sizable amount of the offerings were restricted by donors to missions and can be spent on nothing else.*
>
> • *Revenues may be "inflated" by including interfund transfers in the tithes and offering line and conveniently "**forgetting**" to make the necessary eliminating entries.*
>
> • *Occasionally, when a church's borrowing reaches large levels, a bank may place a restrictive covenant in the loan agreement prohibiting further borrowing. To get around this restriction a church may be inclined to engage in a capital lease, and fail to include the liability on the church balance sheet. To further cover up the trail, the corresponding lease payments are "**buried**" in a repairs and maintenance general ledger account.*

However, fraudulent financial reporting is not limited to phony numbers. Many fraudsters in a position of trust can do just as much damage by leaving things out of financial reports as by putting phony information in. For instance, a business administrator with something to hide, may resort to presenting budget reports generated by electronic spreadsheet software. Since spreadsheets are detached from the church's accounting software, they can easily be manipulated to cover up *"indiscretions."*

Corruption...Is it really that bad?

The Association of Certified Fraud Examiners uses a very strong word to describe a second type of occupational fraud: *corruption*. Few people think of a church when the word corruption is used. Instead, the word conjures up images of Watergate or Al Capone! It appears the Certified Fraud Examiners really want to get a message across.

Referring to a dictionary for a definition of "corruption" does not give much comfort either. A cursory search yields terms like moral perversion, depravity, perversion of integrity, dishonest proceedings, and debased. Since these characteristics rarely occur in a congregation, the first impulse may be to underestimate the potential for corruption fraud to take place in churches.

That would be a mistake, because even though the Fraud Examiners use such a strong word, I believe what the ACFE has in mind can be defined by using another word: bribery. Bribery is "offering something of value to influence a business decision."[2] Unfortunately, this type of behavior can and does take place in churches.

Bribery may or may not be a criminal offense; this depends on local law. But, with churches, that is not the point. This type of behavior is detrimental to a church and in some cases can cause irreparable damage.

Two basic types of bribery are kickbacks and bid-rigging. Of the two, kickbacks are probably the most common method inflicted on churches. Kickbacks consist of giving or transferring anything of value in order to influence a business decision, without the knowledge of the employer or other responsible party. For example, an employee of a church who has been given purchase approval responsibilities might direct orders to his brother-in-law's company in exchange for a "bonus" or "commission." In more severe cases, a compromised purchasing

[2] Ibid., 1.701

agent may submit inflated or fictitious invoices for payment, in exchange for cash or other benefits forwarded to him by the "vendor." At the very minimum, a purchasing agent may exercise poor judgment by paying much higher prices than the market because he is receiving "gifts" for his kindness in directing business to a vendor.

And the winner is...

Far and away, the most common form of fraud in the church environment, and the type of behavior most of us think of when we hear the word fraud, is the *misappropriation of assets*. Or to put it plainly; stealing. As with the other types of bad behavior, crooks use a variety of methods to take what does not belong to them. Asset misappropriation usually falls into three basic categories; cash receipt scams, phony cash disbursements and the theft of non-cash assets.

Generally, two terms are used to describe frauds involving an organization's cash receipts: *skimming* and *larceny*. The difference between the two methods is the timing of the fraud. The process of stealing money before it is recorded in the accounts of the church is called *skimming*. A classic example of church skimming is an usher removing cash from the offering plate on his way to the counting room. On the other hand, if the usher removes money from the bank bag on his way to the bank, *after* the funds have been counted and recorded in the church's records, he has committed *larceny*. *Cash larceny* tends to be a little more difficult because it usually requires "record doctoring" in order for the thief to cover his tracks. Because most churches tend to look closely over the Sunday offerings, thieves' favorite targets for this type of behavior tend to be other revenue sources, such as food service cash boxes, weekday drop-off and mail receipts, and fund raising cash managed by volunteers.

Fraudulent cash disbursements, on the other hand, require much more creativity and planning. These types of transactions involve an employee or volunteer distributing cash to himself or others for dishonest purposes. Unless the organization has absolutely no control over its finances, fraudulent cash disbursements require some form of cover-up or deception in order for the perpetrator to remain anonymous. As a result, a high degree of creativity and imagination is usually required. Despite the extra effort it takes, cash disbursement fraud is probably the most common form of malfeasance among churches.

Some of the more popular disbursement scams are: forging or altering checks, submission and payment of fictitious invoices; inclusion of personal credit card statements with church's statements; "doctored" payroll time cards to increase hours worked (and ultimately pay); creation of "phantom" employees; falsifying expense reports; using the church's credit cards for personal expenses and using church gas cards for personal travel.

There is an interesting fact in regard to non-cash asset thefts. These assets, usually televisions, computers, musical instruments and sound equipment are never stolen. They are just borrowed! The truth is, if a church doesn't watch them closely, these types of assets tend to grow legs and walk away. One other concern in regard to "borrowing" assets is that in the world of tax-exempt organizations, borrowing for personal use can be just as significant a problem as outright theft. Every nonprofit organization's tax exempt status depends on the fact that none of its assets are used for personal purposes. Unreported, excessive, improper personal use of assets like cars, planes, and lodges for example, can result in consequences far more grim than simply losing money.

28

Well, what do we do now?

One challenge in writing a book about church fraud is that the topic may be too alarming. The information may seem overly negative. On the other hand, maybe it needs to be alarming; at least enough to encourage churches to take action. The threat is real, it is dangerous and churches need to start doing something about it. So, the next logical question is this; what should a church do first?

If the Confederate commanders at Gettysburg had taken a little more time to let the smoke clear, they might have been able to gain a better understanding of what they were up against. Then, appropriate steps could have been taken that could have saved the lives of thousands of men.

The first step in fraud prevention is similar. Before rushing into a frontal assault on fraud, time should first be taken in order to slowly, and deliberately analyze the situation. Then, with good information in hand, strong counter measures can be taken to defend the church against this threat. One way to start is for the church to ask itself some probing questions.

Ten questions

The purpose of this book is to help churches add an important element to their financial stewardship practices. In addition to using wisdom in the use of assets, good stewardship requires churches to use wisdom in their *protection* as well. One way of doing this is performing a fraud risk assessment and implementing fraud prevention measures, thus decreasing the likelihood of loss due to occupational fraud. This book is an attempt to help churches begin this process.

The book is organized around ten questions churches should ask themselves. Each question represents a key "brick in the wall" of protection against fraud. The questions are arranged in the order that they should be approached, starting with developing an organizational structure resistant to fraud and ending with a formal commitment and process of maintaining vigilance in the war against a strengthening foe.

Chapter 3

How Strong Is Your Batting Order?

(The Essential Role of Organizational Structure)

"Moses listened to his father-in-law and did everything he said. He chose capable men from all Israel and made them leaders of the people, officials over thousands, hundreds, fifties and tens."

Exodus 18:24-25, New International Version

Principle – Churches that put little thought into their organizational structure are frequent targets of fraud.

From March to October, if a baseball game is on television I am watching it, or at least listening on radio if I am working. There is no better background music than a baseball play-by-play announcer.

With the exception of the holidays, from the conclusion of the World Series in late October until mid-February is my least favorite part of the year. I am not very fond of the winter months but not because of cold weather. It is the absence of baseball that bugs me the most! I am a baseball fan.

Most people believe baseball is no longer our national pastime. But, that does not faze me in the least. I still think baseball is the greatest game and I love almost everything about it. (Except the Yankees of course!)

One of the things particularly appealing to me is the strategy of the game which begins well before the umpire yells, "Play ball!" For example, baseball managers lose sleep and sweat blood over setting their line-up cards and there is good reason for their anxiety. How the batting order is arranged has a huge impact on the outcome of the game.

Setting a batting order seems to be as much art as science since a multitude of factors influence the decision. In addition to keeping up with batting averages and on-base percentages, managers must also consider their players' health, personalities, and huge egos. And, there are no athletes more superstitious than baseball players. Once the manager gets through all of this, he can then place his nine players into their assigned roles. Each spot in the order has a defined role and players are assigned their slots according to their ability to fulfill that role.

A baseball manager's job is to assess his team and arrange his players in an order that gives the team the best chance to win. If the manager is good at this exercise, he enhances his chances for success; otherwise the game may be lost before it starts.

Churches are faced with similar challenges. Those that plan ahead and lay down a strong organizational structure, a line-up card if you will, increase their chances of avoiding costly, rally-killing mistakes. However, those who don't organize well will face difficulties. They will be subject to inefficiencies, discouragement, stunted growth, dissensions, and lack of focus which will probably result in the failure of a church to carry out its mission. And adding injury to insult, when the organizational structure is weak, a church is much more likely to be victimized by fraud. It is imperative, before any basic fraud prevention measures are taken, that a church spends whatever time and effort is necessary, to organize itself in a way to put its best line-up on the field.

Character matters...

Effective organization starts at the top. In fact, the first thing auditors, potential donors, granting agencies and IRS agents try to determine is the quality of an organization's *"tone at the top."* The first ingredient of good tone at the top is attitude, particularly the attitude of the senior leadership of a church. This is the first brick that must be placed in the wall of fraud protection. It may be the most important brick too. If there is no desire to do things right and operate with integrity and openness, then there are no amount of checks and balances that will be effective. Any controls put in place will simply be ignored or willfully overridden.

Even in a church, tone at the top does not happen by accident. It begins with a desire by the church leadership, (executive level employees and lay leaders) to operate in transparency. To instill a healthy tone at the top, a concerted effort must be taken that includes communicating on a regular basis the need for accountability in all areas of the church, as well as the values the church expects its representatives to model. Church leadership should also make an open statement of its commitment to transparency by participating in accountability measures such as requiring all individuals in positions of trust to sign conflict of interest statements. Most importantly, the church must insist that these trusted individuals live by the church's accountability rules.

Teamwork...

The next step in organization involves the conversion of the attitude into action. The tone at the top should be converted from words to the establishment of an appropriate and effective organizational frame-work. The first step is the creation of an effective "Leadership Team." [1] Before filling out a line-up card (assigning people to tasks), each church should take sufficient time to carefully create a leadership team that will give it the best chance of success in carrying out its mission while at the same time providing accountability to its congregation. An effective leadership team should have several key characteristics:

---

[1] Terminology varies from church to church. I am using "leadership team" interchangeably with board of elders, finance committee, trustees, etc.

- **Formal** – *A leadership team should be* **formally** *established. It should be created by the church as both the authoritative* **and** *responsible decision making body. The choice of governance should be clearly communicated to the congregation.*

- **Representative** – *The leadership team should be elected or appointed in such a way as to be a good representation of the church. Selecting leaders in this manner allows the church to benefit from the multitude of gifts present in the congregation.*

- **Empowered** – *The team must not be "for show," but should be given authority to ask "difficult" or "uncomfortable" questions and make crucial decisions.*

- **Competent** – *The team should be made of individuals skilled and gifted in ways that help the church accomplish its mission. The members should consist of individuals gifted or experienced in finance, nonprofit organization management, personnel matters and ministry.*

- **Accountable** – *The team must keep good records of its meetings and decisions and keep the congregation clearly informed of the activities of the church.*

- **Servant leadership** – *The team members must clearly understand that their role is to* **serve** *their church not to rule it.*

If the lead dog won't run...

A good plan and a good leadership team are not enough, because even with those two elements, if there has been no *staff buy-in* to the process, success will prove elusive. If senior level church staff is not committed to accountability and transparency, it will be very difficult for any fraud protection measures to be effective. Keep in mind that if administrative matters are not important to the employees at the top, they will not be important to the rank and file as well. The net effect will be a weakening of the church's defenses from top to bottom. The entire organizational structure of the church will be "softened up" for an embezzler to work his craft.

Some of the key characteristics indicating that the staff has bought in to a spirit of accountability can be obtained by addressing the following questions:

> • *Are transparency and integrity important to senior staff, or do they simply pay lip service to them?*
>
> • *How supportive is senior staff of administrative policies and decisions of the finance office?*
>
> • *Do senior ministers cooperate willingly with administrative duties, such as submitting expense reports on a timely basis? Or, do they complain loudly and openly?*
>
> • *Do senior ministers respect the law and insist upon complying with it?*

Winning with volunteers...

The church is the ultimate volunteer organization and has been so for almost two thousand years. By far, the majority of the work carried out in a local church is performed by the laity. Without volunteers the church would be in serious trouble.

Unfortunately, many churches do their volunteers a great disservice by throwing them into the battle well before they are ready. Much too often the "tyranny of the urgent" forces volunteers into the front lines with little or no preparation. Also, in this haste, churches may place individuals in a place of trust where they do not belong. After a nightmare that has lasted more than twenty years, it is rare to find a church that does not perform a criminal background check on its child care workers. But, a growing number of churches are coming to regret not taking the time to check the financial backgrounds of individuals wishing to serve as volunteers in financial tasks.

The result of this failing to screen and train volunteers is "mistakes" may occur that can take a heavy toll on a church; financially, emotionally, and spiritually. Having inadequately trained volunteers often leads to mistakes in judgment which can prove to be very costly. Even worse, poor management of volunteers can also lead to the presence of financial predators who will take advantage of the church and its members. To operate effectively and safely, churches should use care in placing volunteers in the church's batting order. Two key ingredients are training and screening.

Conclusion...

Successful baseball managers have an intense desire to win. They spend hours sweating over their starting lineup. To get an edge over their opponents, they look intensely for a perfect combination of speed, power, defense and instinct for the game. When they find it, they often get to play baseball in October.

Churches should be just as passionate about establishing their organizational line-ups. They should do this not to get an edge over anyone, but to be good stewards. Churches should look for their perfect combination of executive employees, leadership team and volunteers.

Not only will this dedication to organization result in efficiency and effectiveness; the organizational structure put in place will serve as a deterrent to potential financial predators.

Recent headlines...
(Names have been changed to protect the innocent; and the guilty!)

Those pesky pastor's discretionary funds

> "The long time pastor of St. Mark's church has been ousted by his congregation amid accusations of improperly taking money from his discretionary account over a period of years. The pastor is expected to be formally fired from St. Mark's today when the congregation will ask the assembly to dissolve his relationship with the church."

If only this church had...let the chairman of the deacons share responsibility with the pastor for the fund's administration.

A thousand here, a thousand there, pretty soon we're talking real money...

"THE REVEREND JOHN JONES OF PLEASANT VALLEY COMMUNITY CHURCH, HIS WIFE AND ASSOCIATE PASTOR, HAVE BEEN ACCUSED BY THE DISTRICT ATTORNEY, OF STEALING $495,500."

If only this church... had an independent board or leadership team to assist in the church's stewardship rather than giving complete and total operational control to the senior employees.

Volunteers aren't in it for the money...Or are they?

"A LOCAL MAN WHO VOLUNTEERED TO COUNT THE WEEKLY OFFERINGS AT FIRST COMMUNITY CHURCH HAS BEEN CHARGED WITH EMBEZZLEMENT. THIRTY FIVE YEAR OLD ROBERT SMITH WAS ARRESTED AND CHARGED WITH FELONY LARCENY IN AN AMOUNT EXCEEDING $500. POLICE SAY THAT MR. SMITH HAS BEEN A VOLUNTEER TELLER FOR MORE THAN FIVE YEARS. CHURCH OFFICIALS BECAME ALARMED WHEN THEY NOTICED A DROP OFF IN COLLECTIONS EACH TIME MR. SMITH SERVED ON THE COUNT TEAM."

If only this church...held periodical formal volunteer orientation retreats (where job requirements and expectations were clearly communicated) and conducted thorough volunteer screening.

Five point fraud prevention test...

- Has your church developed and implemented a formal staff orientation and training program?

- Does your church have a formal leadership team?

- Does your leadership team meet on a regular basis, keep minutes of its actions, and is it representative of the church congregation?

- Does your church provide formal orientation and training for its volunteers, especially those in high-exposure tasks such as child care and financial management?

- Does your church periodically review its leadership structure, internal controls and management policies?

Are You a Church Without Walls?

Chapter 4

Are You a Church Without Walls?

If the owner of the house had known at what time of night the thief was coming, he would have kept watch and would not have let his house be broken into.

Matthew 24:43-44, New International Version

Principle – Corporate documents and written policies and procedures serve as a protective "wall" guarding a church from fraud.

Jerusalem was a mess. After years of rebellion and failure to heed the warnings given by God's prophets, judgment had finally come. Judah had been brought to its knees by the wrath of King Nebuchadnezzar and the Babylonians. Jerusalem was sacked and the best and brightest of the nation exiled to Babylon. The rest were slaughtered or left to live off the land.

But, in the revolving door of Middle-Eastern politics, nothing lasts forever. Within the lifetimes of some of the original exiles, the Persians wrestled control away from the Babylonians. Cyrus, the King of Persia, issued an edict allowing the Jews, at least those who wanted to, to return to their homeland. After one failed attempt, a new temple was finally dedicated by Zerubbabel in 515 B.C.

More than fifty years later, Nehemiah, the Jewish cupbearer to the Persian King, asked his brother about the state of the beloved city. The report was not good as Jerusalem continued to lie in ruins. The once mighty city was helpless to defend itself against enemy armies. In fact, Jerusalem could not even defend itself against wild animals because the city gates had been burned. But even if the gates had survived, they would have been useless because there was nothing to attach them to: the city's walls were in shambles.

The people were not in much better shape either. With no walls for protection, in addition to being defenseless, they felt a deep sense of disgrace. The Jewish people, proud descendants and inheritors of the heroics of King David and the wealth and wisdom of King Solomon, had been reduced to a subsistence lifestyle. And with the disgrace came discouragement and apathy. As a result, Jerusalem continued to lie in ruins.

Nehemiah the wall builder

In the midpoint of the fifth century, the nation's two most influential men since Solomon rode on the stage – Ezra and Nehemiah. Each had a significant but different role in the restoration of the nation. Ezra, the spiritual leader, came to Jerusalem with his dreams and reforms raising the hopes of the people from the ashes. And, a few years later Nehemiah, a devout Jewish government official, arrived with the vision of rebuilding his broken city.

Nehemiah has long been looked upon as the "gold standard" in exemplifying leadership principles because of the steps he took in rebuilding Jerusalem. First, Nehemiah did not act rashly and impulsively: his initial step was a simple midnight stroll. Nehemiah quietly and discretely walked the city of Jerusalem in an effort to gain an understanding of the situation. When he had completed his tour, Nehemiah had a working understanding of what needed to be accomplished first: life in Jerusalem could not return to normal until the walls were replaced.

Next, Nehemiah reduced the larger task into manageable portions and delegated the work to others. Various sections of the walls were assigned to those who lived or worked close to the areas they were given responsibility for. Nehemiah matched the work to the workers and the assignments resulted in immediate "buy-in" by his followers. This, along with Nehemiah's frequent words of encouragement, began to raise the hopes of his people.

However, Nehemiah's work was not without opposition. Two individuals named Sanballat and Tobiah, had a big problem with what was about to take place and they made it their goal to stop the work. For some reason, these two found it offensive that "someone had come to promote the welfare of the Israelites."[1] Their behavior is not unlike some church members who have no suggestions of their own, but seem to enjoy tearing down the work of others.

Sanballat, Tobiah and their friends entered into a campaign of slander by mocking and ridiculing Nehemiah and the others engaged in the rebuilding. They sought every effort to stir up trouble in order to impede the work, going so far as boasting, "We will be right there among you."[2] Sanballat also tried to distract Nehemiah by requesting a meeting to discuss the work.

But, Nehemiah and the others were not fazed by the opposition. They continued diligently in their work to rebuild protective walls around the city. And their efforts were rewarded with staggering success. The walls were completed in record time – fifty-two days. The city was now protected and work on rebuilding the rest of the infrastructure could proceed rapidly. At long last, the citizens of Jerusalem could rest a little easier.

[1]Nehemiah 2:10. New International Version
[2]Nehemiah 4:11

Of equal importance however is the impact Nehemiah's success had on his enemies. "When all our enemies heard about this, all the surrounding nations were afraid and lost their self-confidence, because they realized that this work had been done with the help of our God."[3]

Comparison: The sacking of Jerusalem and the sacking of a church...

A parallel can be drawn between Jerusalem, sacked and broken down, and a church hit by fraud or embezzlement. Similar to ancient Jerusalem, the aftermath of a financial scandal can devastate a church. In fact, if not kept in check, the aftermath can be more damaging in the long-run than the original financial loss. With its protective financial walls burned and broken down to ground level, a church could find itself defenseless *and*, in worse-case situations, in financial ruin. The effects can linger for years. Unfortunately, some churches never recover.

Nehemiah described his people as "disgraced," which is exactly the feeling many members and staff have at churches victimized by fraud. This emotion probably explains why so many cases of church embezzlement go unreported; it is just too embarrassing to admit that "it happened here."

However, the most painful wound fraud incident may well be the *discouragement* that takes up residence in the hearts of the people of the church. Discouragement will affect a church at both the corporate and the individual levels. Corporately, the vision of the church may never be carried out because the "incident" has deflated the desire of the congregation as a community to reach their goals.

The individual impact is even more serious. Some people may leave the church over what they have seen. Far worse, some individuals may become so discouraged they may even leave the faith because of the terrible role model they have witnessed. This last reason alone makes it imperative that every church build a protective wall to ward off the dangers lined up against it. Lives are at stake!

They still don't get it...

In spite of these implications, many churches never take the time to build a protective "wall" for their church by developing, documenting and implementing written policies and procedures, (including fraud assessment and protection measures) to guide the congregation. Many reasons are given for this failure, but the three most common are limited staff size, inadequate resources and lack of time.

However, a more troubling reason may be the cause; the presence of modern-day Sanballats and Tobiahs in the congregation. Suggestions to improve processes may be met with ridicule. Even when a few "baby" steps are taken, out of the blue will come a Sanballat to sabotage the process.

These obstacles can be overcome by simply following the pattern set by Nehemiah. He clearly understood the dangerous nature of the world he lived in, but refused to let fear or opposition paralyze him. Church administrators should also move ahead, but cautiously, just as

Nehemiah did. Before plunging in, like Nehemiah, they should take a stroll around the church's processes to gain an understanding of the dangers they may be facing.

Like Nehemiah they should not do it alone. Competent, interested and dedicated people should be enlisted and the work delegated among them. Delegation not only increases efficiency it also enhances the probability of staff "buy-in." Strength in numbers helps the business administrator ignore the distractive nature of opposition. Distraction can cause as much trouble as destruction.

When the wall is completed, the church and its ministry will be safer. And just like the Bible story, the enemies of the church will be afraid: afraid of being caught that is. They will lose their "self-confidence." Before attacking the well-defended church the potential financial predator will be forced to stop and ask himself; "Do I feel lucky?" or "Do I need to move on to a church that has not protected itself?"

How to build a wall...

Let's be specific. How exactly is a wall of protection built? Once again, Nehemiah can serve as our role model."

Assess the situation. Before taking any dramatic steps, a church's current state of fraud prevention readiness must be determined. Typically, this is accomplished through inquiry and observation. Interviewing staff, leadership team members, and key volunteers to obtain their impressions is a good first step. To broaden the scope, and perhaps obtain more forthcoming answers, distributing questionnaires to staff and volunteers might be considered. Additionally, keeping the responses confidential enhances the effectiveness of the information obtained. The assessment phase of the process should be a broad overview of what's going on, not a detailed analysis at the transaction level. Some of the questions to answer are:

- *Does the church have any policies at all, either written or verbal?*

- *If the church does have policies, have they been adequately documented?*

- *Does the church implement the policies and use them on a daily basis?*

- *If the church has written policies, have they been compiled in a central document that is readily available to employees and lay leaders?*

- *If written policies exist, are they well- written, up-to-date and comprehensive?*

- *If the church has a policy manual, is it reviewed and updated periodically?*

Build a Team. Don't be the Lone Ranger, because you will not win. Build a team to help develop the plan by using the following techniques:

- Like Nehemiah, the best approach is to delegate the work in bite-size sections to a sufficient number of team members.

- Encourage and build enthusiasm among the team members.

- Teach and train team members so that they can understand the seriousness of the matter.

- Bring an understanding that the effort is a spiritual exercise; another form of stewardship.

- Include a strong mechanism for feedback and reporting.

Be deliberate and determined in approach. Build the wall, brick by brick.

- From the results of the initial assessment try to anticipate things that could go wrong.

- Develop policies to address the concerns.

- **Put the plan in writing.**

- Be thorough, but concise. (Try to cover all areas. The response to each area should be short and directly to the point. What is not needed is a federal government-sized code book. Just clear guidelines.)

- **Compile the policy in a central document.**

Use the right materials. What should the wall be made of? Because each congregation has its own unique culture, a great deal of variation exists between churches. Some of the topics that should be in every church's protective wall are as follows:

- *Organization and governance* – If a church does not have a formal and well documented organizational structure, its ability to ward off financial abuse is severely weakened. If no clear structure exists, it will be very difficult to know if anything wrong has taken place. "Normal" has to be clearly defined. To help solidify the authority of the organizational structure mentioned in the previous chapter, it must be clearly defined and documented.

- *Budget development* – Historically, church budgets have had a two-fold purpose. First, they fill a purely financial role helping make sure the church stays within acceptable and approved spending parameters. The church budget also has a spiritual role in that a church budget is simply the congregation's vision for the coming year, stated in dollars. Increasingly, budgets are fulfilling a third purpose: helping prevent and exposing fraudulent behavior. A detailed budget provides a baseline for churches to make comparisons to identify financial variances and anomalies.

- *Cash receipts procedures* – Cash receipts are the financial life-blood of a church and stories of teller/count team shenanigans are legendary. Needless to say, standard policies are essential to guide tithes and offerings to the proper place. This topic will be discussed in detail in a subsequent chapter.

- *Cash disbursement procedures* – *Even though cash receipts improprieties garner more of the headlines, the larger scams seem to involve cash disbursement mismanagement. A strong bill approval and payment system should be documented.*

- *Personnel* – *This is the largest single expenditure of most churches. As a result there is more opportunity for problems here than any other part of a church's operations.*

These are the four basic components of church management that should be included in every church's policy manual. However, there are many more that should find their way into church policy and procedure manuals. Among them are policies governing: investments, fixed assets, risk management, IRS compliance, building use, food service, fraud prevention, and disaster recovery.

Put the policy to use. Once the wall is completed, (the document written) churches sometimes put it on the shelf to gather dust. Needless to say, a policy and procedure document will not provide much protection unless it is used.

- *Make it accessible. Don't let it become the code book of one or two in the church. Instead, freely distribute it though multiple copies or better yet, produce an electronic version.*

- *Have a scheduled maintenance plan. Periodically review and update the document as conditions change.*

Conclusion...

Nehemiah's amazing and miraculous fifty-two day construction project had an immediate and dramatic effect. It gave the remnant of Judah protection and a renewed confidence in their future. However, the impact of Nehemiah's wall building had a much more important impact.

Approximately five hundred years later, on what we now call Palm Sunday, Israel's Messiah rode through the streets of the city Nehemiah rebuilt. Nehemiah's wall helped prepare the way for God's plan of redemption.

When a church builds a figurative wall of fraud protection, it is doing a similar thing. By reducing the possibility of fraud, a church can free itself from distractions. The church will then be freed up to carry out its part in God's plan of reaching out to men and women.

Recent headlines...

think the horses are already out of the corral...

"AN EMPLOYEE OF MAPLE VIEW COMMUNITY CHURCH WAS ARRESTED SATURDAY AND CHARGED WITH STEALING MORE THAN $175,000 FROM THE CHURCH, POLICE SAID. THE CHURCH BOOKKEEPER HAS BEEN CHARGED WITH THEFT IN CONNECTION WITH THE EMBEZZLEMENT. "EVERYBODY LIKED AND RESPECTED HER, AND THERE ARE A LOT OF EMOTIONS RUNNING THROUGH THE CHURCH RIGHT NOW." CHURCH

LEADERS SAID THE LOSS AMOUNTS TO MORE THAN A THIRD OF THE CHURCH'S ANNUAL BUDGET. THEY ALSO SAID 'THEY PLAN TO DEVELOP A SYSTEM OF CHECKS AND BALANCES IN THEIR ACCOUNTING SYSTEMS'..."

*If only this church had...implemented **written** internal accounting controls, **before** hiring this trusted employee*

So, what are you thinking now?

"CHURCH MEMBERS ARE IN A STATE OF SHOCK SINCE LEARNING THAT A LONG-TIME MEMBER HAS BEEN CHARGED WITH STEALING MORE THAN $25,000 FROM THE SUNDAY COLLECTIONS OF MOUNT CARMEL CHURCH. A CHURCH SPOKESMAN COMMENTED THAT, "IN CHURCHES, WE TRUST OUR PEOPLE A LITTLE TOO MUCH. YOU WOULDN'T THINK A CHURCH PERSON WOULD EMBEZZLE, SO WE DON'T HAVE MANY INTERNAL CONTROLS..."

*If only this church had...implemented written volunteer counting procedures prohibiting any one individual to be in possession of church funds for **any** period of time, no matter how short a duration.*

In order for budgets to work, they have to be looked at...

"ACCORDING TO NEWS REPORTS, AN EMPLOYEE OF SUNSET CHURCH EMBEZZLED MORE THAN $100,000 FROM THE CHURCH'S GENERAL OPERATING FUND OVER A PERIOD OF EIGHTEEN MONTHS. THE DISCOVERY OCCURRED WHEN THE FINANCE COUNCIL BEGAN LOOKING INTO DISCREPANCIES IN THE CHURCH BUDGET REPORT NOTICED BY A MEMBER OF

THE CONGREGATION. THE FINANCE CHAIRMAN COMMENTED
THAT 'I WISH WE HAD LOOKED AT THE BUDGET REPORTS A
LITTLE EARLIER'."

*If only this church had...provided budget versus actual
reports, **monthly** to their finance team who had the
authority to question variations or anomalies.*

Five point fraud prevention test...

> • *Does your church have up-to-date corporate documents
>   and are they periodically reviewed by legal counsel
>   experienced in nonprofit law?*
>
> • *Has your church written a thorough but concise policy,
>   procedures and processes manual?*
>
> • *Has the church made the document readily accessible to
>   staff, leadership team members and key volunteers?*
>
> • *Is the document periodically reviewed to make sure it is
>   up-to-date?*
>
> • *Does your church adopt an annual budget which is
>   routinely compared to actual results?*

Weeds in the Garden

Are You a Geek?
Maybe You Should Be!

You know how to interpret the appearance of the sky, but you cannot interpret the signs of the times.

Matthew 16:3, New International Version

Principle – Churches that do not keep in step with the constant change in information technology may experience firsthand the dangers of the brave new "digital" world.

I am no historian, so what I am about to say can certainly be challenged by those more knowledgeable about such things. But when I look at the state of affairs when the Civil War began, it seems to me that the ultimate outcome should have never been in doubt.

The nineteenth century can be described using one word: change, and most, if not all of these changes, favored the northern states. Changing demographics and economic realities weighed heavily in favor of the North. For instance, the states remaining faithful to the Union held more than a two to one advantage over the South in population. Added to this population advantage was an enormous and rapidly expanding industrial base which enabled the North to supply war materials, seemingly without end. Of equal importance, this industrial base provided immense wealth which allowed the North to not only fight a war, but to finance one as well.

Due to rapidly changing technology, the Union also had logistical advantages. The nation's ongoing project of developing a unified, coast-to-coast rail system provided tremendous efficiencies in transporting war materials. Along side of the tracks, thousands of miles of telegraph cable were strung creating a communication system that contributed to a well-coordinated war effort.

Although more subtle in nature, changes of a more philosophical and moral nature assisted the North in the war effort. The concept of fighting for "union" strengthened the North. But, while the South's strong belief in "states' rights" provided a rallying cry to encourage troops and citizens, it also occasionally led to sectional disagreements. Lack of consensus in time of war can prove fatal.

Cultural changes were taking place as well. At the outbreak of the Civil War, Southern culture *and* economics were based on an agricultural way of life. On the surface this does not sound so bad. Today, many city-dwellers long for the slower and simpler rural way of life but, the agricultural system in place in the South in the 1850s was antiquated and lurching towards extinction. To a large extent, the Southern economy was based on the plantation system heavily favoring the wealthy, excluding all blacks but, also most whites as well. What is both a mystery of the War and a testimony to love of the Homeland is how many poor Southern soldiers, with little or no vested economic interest in the Southern economic system, were so willing to sacrifice their lives.

Significant moral and social trends also significantly favored the North. Slavery was becoming a pariah and freedom was on the rise around the world. *Individual* initiative and a desire to improve *personal* standards of living were becoming desires of many. Even without the Civil War, the plantation system and slavery were probably headed for extinction.

Nineteenth century America was in a state of change: technologically, demographically, economically, philosophically, morally and spiritually. The North took note of the changes and put them to their advantage, but only after some very costly hesitation. On the other hand, the South might not have even noticed. As a result, they marched off to war not knowing what was about to happen to them.

Parallels to the church...

Churches must be careful not to make the same mistake. They need to understand the twenty-first century is characterized by the same word: change. More importantly, churches need to know that this change has a direct impact on how a church does its business.

The risks of not recognizing changes are significant and come in many different forms. For example, in the last twenty-five years the United States has gone through tremendous *demographic* change. As a result, due to immigration, birth rates and an aging population, the membership of many churches is not representative of the neighborhood in which their church is located. Failing to recognize this demographic change early enough has led to a long, slow death for many churches, planted during the early years of the baby boom. Recognizing demographic change earlier could have allowed these churches to develop effective outreach ministries and stave off extinction.

Economic change is another factor churches must clearly understand in order to exercise the best stewardship. The dizzying volatility of today's financial markets requires that churches stay up to date in their understanding of economic and financial trends. Decisions delayed by just a few hours can result in costly consequences.

But, there is another source of change that is of extreme importance, which is also enhancing fraudsters' ability to do their dirty work. As a result, churches also must come to grips with the "speed of light" change in technology. While most churches understand that things are changing rapidly, they may have failed to fully grabble with the implications this change has on the way they use their computers.

Computers help accomplish so much...

Information technology (IT) and fraud prevention should be a concern to all churches, regardless of size. Manual accounting and bookkeeping systems are pretty much a thing of the past. Even the smallest churches depend on computers to keep up with their finances using software from the less expensive but wildly popular QuickBooks© to more expensive, church-specific software management systems.

In addition to financial reporting and contributions record-keeping, churches are using their computers in a multiplicity of applications. Computer applications are used to enhance childcare security through sophisticated check-in procedures; accept tithes and offerings online and at fancy kiosks in the church lobby; and purchase supplies online. Many churches are sharpening the focus of their outreach efforts with the assistance of expanded member data base applications. Others are providing free Wi-Fi service in their lobbies in an attempt to attract "seekers."

Computers also bring their own set of problems...

Without a doubt, churches, particularly the larger ones, have jumped feet-first into the brave new technology world. Unfortunately, many are doing so not knowing that there may be snakes in the pond! Carried away with excitement over the latest new "upgrade," very few churches take the time to "upgrade" their fraud protection measures. The result: even though they may be getting a lot more done, more efficiently and at a lower cost, they may have opened doors to the cyber world that can cause them to suffer irreparable damage.

For their own financial health, churches need to understand the *full implications* of living in this brave new world of technology. While computers have enhanced productivity and effectiveness beyond our wildest imaginations, it needs to be kept in mind that the digital world brings challenges as well. One of the most significant challenges is the new types of fraud that can be encountered. One thing is certain: churches may not be aware of the vast changes in technology, but the crooks are, and they are putting these changes to work.

Inside jobs...

Usually a church's first concerns in regard to computer fraud are *internal* threats.

In years past, before computers, much of the church record keeping was performed manually. Because doing things manually takes such a long time, much of the record keeping of a church was distributed among several people out of necessity. But today, with the assistance

59

of computers, one individual can be involved in many, (unfortunately, in some cases all!) aspects of the church fiscal activities. Often, after a transition from manual to electronic financial management, too many of the financial tasks wind up concentrated with one individual.

In fact, it is not unusual to find churches who have invested heavily in church management software with the following set of circumstances:

> - *A financial secretary or bookkeeper who has access to all of the church management system's modules. (Cash receipts and contributions, member records, bank reconciliation, accounts payable, etc.)*
>
> - *Passwords are considered a nuisance by church staff and are shared or are extremely simple resulting in almost unlimited access to the church's information.*
>
> - *Information back-ups are not professionally performed. It is not uncommon for some churches to have no back-up at all. Some have back-up but only at the home of IT staff or a volunteer. This may work well until the IT guy suddenly gets mad and joins another church.*

When too much access and control is concentrated in one individual, segregation of accounting and management duties becomes very difficult. The reliability of a church's records will then be subject to the strength, character and ability of the individual who has all of the controls at his or her disposal. Poor accounting and managerial skills can result in inaccurate reporting which can lead to poor decision-making by the church.

But, poor ethical *skills* can result in something far worse than incorrect reports. A combination of unlimited access to financial records, tasks and responsibilities concentrated in one individual and lack of integrity can lead to a nightmare situation; embezzlement of church funds.

High-tech break-ins...

The area where churches may be the most naïve are cyber threats from outside the walls of the church. Few give enough thought to a basic twenty-first century fact of life; by opening one single internet account, if care is not exercised, the world has been invited into your living room. Today, except for the very smallest of congregations, all churches are vulnerable to hackers wanting to take advantage of the perceived, and in many cases real naïveté of churches.

Most churches, at the very least, have Internet access. In addition, it seems the vast majority of churches have taken it a step further by developing their own web-sites, many of which are "interactive." While being "interactive" is a good way to minister to church members and reach out to the unchurched, it must be kept in mind that this practice may also let the "bad" in with the good.

Churches also make online purchases, sell goods and event tickets online, and an increasing number receive offerings online. Without question these steps have improved the efficiency and effectiveness of churches. Using fewer staff and volunteers and spending much less time, churches can do a better job of collecting and tabulating gifts, managing church activities, reporting results, and most importantly, reaching out to the unchurched. However, each of these new ways of doing business represents a new porthole through which fraudsters can gain entrance to church data and assets.

Cyber crime is serious and is growing rapidly. Some of these criminal activities have a point, they are crimes carried out by people who simply want to take something that is not theirs. But others make very little sense because they seem to have no other purpose than to simply destroy and create mayhem.

Pointless, pointless, pointless...

One such "pointless" threat is *malware*. Malware is *malicious* software designed to specifically damage or disrupt a computer system. Often, the only ingredient necessary for making this threat a reality is simply logging on to the Internet. These programs can cause incalculable damage and the irony is that in most cases the perpetrator is not even present to take pride in his work. What is the point?

There are three primary means by which malware can gain entrance to a church's financial system. In one way or another, each of the three is some form of "invitation" that someone at the church may have answered. First is *spam, or unsolicited emails.* Much of this may come from legitimate sources and sites visited by church staff, but others can be totally "out of the blue." The best protection is making sure church staff knows not to "invite" potential malware into the church house by opening emails from unknown sources.

Malware can also knock on your door through *emails* from "good" sources like members and vendors. The problem is that these friends of the church may not be as diligent in protecting their own systems.

The third primary method of entrance, and a very frequent culprit in the church environment are *downloads*. Many churches have learned the hard way that with any download some unwanted, harmful, damaging and intrusive bonus features may also arrive.

Software fraud with a point...

Even though "pointless" computer threats can be costly and painful, they in no way compare with the damage that can be done by cyber fraudsters operating with a purpose; stealing from the church. Any church, regardless of size, has something of immense economic value. Even though the church cannot sell and convert its database into cash, the information can be worth millions of dollars to identity thieves. Many churches have within their management systems much of the information hackers need to do their work: names, addresses, phone numbers, email addresses, social security numbers and in some cases banking information.

Having this information is nothing new; for many years churches have maintained physical files of this type of information. For example, many church's giving records consisted of copies of member checks which in the wrong hands could result in economic calamity. In the past, to get to this information, thieves had to break into the church to gain access to the files. But no longer is this the case; they can simply sit at their computer, do their work, and make a fortune.

Conclusion...

Churches need to remember what the South forgot: the world has changed. Although in many ways computers and the Internet have made life much easier, they have also presented new challenges. Churches need to recognize the changes that have taken place and develop strong Information Technology policies and processes. This will provide protection for the church's assets, reputation and most importantly, the church's ability to continue its ministry.

Recent headlines...

"Taking from Caesar what is Caesar's..."

A "TRUSTED" CHURCH ACCOUNTANT WAS GIVEN ACCESS TO ALL OF THE MODULES OF HIS CHURCH'S DATA MANAGEMENT SYSTEM. ADDITIONALLY, HIS TASKS INCLUDED ASSISTING IN DEPOSIT PREPARATION AND RECONCILING THE BANK STATE-MENTS. WHEN A NEW ASSISTANT WAS HIRED SHE NOTICED THAT THE TOTAL CASH DEPOSITED WAS CONSISTENTLY LESS THAN THE AMOUNT REPORTED AS OFFERINGS IN THE CHURCH'S CONTRIBUTION MODULE. AFTER FURTHER INVES-TIGATION IT WAS DISCOVERED THAT THE ACCOUNTANT HAD BEEN INFLATING HIS OWN DONATION AMOUNTS IN ORDER TO GENERATE FICTITIOUS TAX DEDUCTIONS.

If this church had only partitioned its accounting soft-ware modules between staff and volunteers prohibit-ing any one individual from having unlimited access.

"Into thin air..."

IN ORDER TO BE "CUTTING EDGE" A CHURCH DECIDED TO BEGIN ACCEPTING GIFTS ONLINE. A THIRD PARTY SERVICE PROVIDER WAS ENGAGED TO ADMINISTER THE ONLINE GIVING ACTIVITIES. FUNDS WERE TRANSMITTED FROM MEMBER BANK ACCOUNTS TO THE SERVICE PROVIDER WHO WOULD THEN FORWARD THE CASH TO THE CHURCH'S BANK ACCOUNT. THE CHURCH WAS HAPPY WITH THE SERVICE WITH ONE EXCEPTION. SOMETHING ABOUT THE REPORTING MECHANISM WAS SOMEWHAT BOTHERSOME. WHILE THE CHURCH WAS PROVIDED WITH A MONTHLY LIST OF GIFTS GIVEN BY MEMBER, NO REPORTS WERE GIVEN THAT COULD BE AGREED TO DEPOSIT AMOUNTS. REPEATED REQUESTS FOR A RECONCILIATION WERE MADE BUT NO SATISFACTORY ANSWERS WERE RECEIVED. EVENTUALLY, AFTER AN EXTENSIVE INVESTIGATION, IT WAS LEARNED THAT EMPLOYEES OF THE SERVICE PROVIDER WERE "SKIMMING" FROM THEIR VARIOUS CLIENTS AND HIDING THEIR ACTIONS BEHIND "POOR REPORTING."

If only this church had insisted on a reporting mechanism from its provider that included a detailed list of contributors

"Nobody likes purchase orders..."

A CHURCH HAD A LONG HISTORY OF EXCEPTIONAL BUSINESS PRACTICES INCLUDING A WELL DEFINED APPROVAL SYSTEM FOR INITIATING PURCHASES OF GOODS AND SERVICES. THE PROCESS WAS ADEQUATELY DOCUMENTED WITH SEQUENTIALLY NUMBERED PURCHASE ORDERS FOR PURCHASES EXCEEDING SPECIFIED AMOUNTS. HOWEVER, ON AN *EMERGENCY* BASIS, THE CHURCH BEGAN BUYING "ONLINE."

ENTICED BY THE EFFICIENCY OF THE CYBER MARKET-
PLACE, THE CHURCH GREATLY EXPANDED ITS ONLINE
PURCHASES BUT FAILED TO "UPDATE" ITS PURCHASING
PROCESSES TO COVER THIS NEW WAY OF DOING BUSINESS.
UNFORTUNATELY, A NEW-HIRE WITH QUESTIONABLE ETHICS
LEARNED OF THIS AND MADE SIGNIFICANT ON-LINE PUR-
CHASES. HE OVERSPENT HIS BUDGET TO SUCH AN EXTENT
THAT BUDGET AMENDMENTS HAD TO BE MADE IN MID-
YEAR, CAUSING A FAIR AMOUNT OF CHURCH DISSENSION
AND DISCUSSION. WORSE, MANY OF THE PURCHASES WERE
FOR PERSONAL ITEMS OF THE MINISTER WHICH ATTRACTED
THE ATTENTION OF LOCAL MEDIA.

*If only this church had a "technology team" charged
with reviewing church practices in regard to technology on at least an annual basis.*

Five point fraud prevention test...

- *Has your church written a detailed Information Technology security plan?*

- *Does your church partition the various modules of its data management software so that no one individual has access to all application modules?*

- *Does the church have a strong password protection system?*

- *Has the church developed any online protection measures against malware, downloads, and unsolicited email dangers?*

- *Does your church take seriously its responsibility to protect the information its members have entrusted it with?*

Weeds in the Garden

Chapter 6

Are You Producing Financial Statements or Spin Documents?

Jesus told his disciples: "There was a rich man whose manager was accused of wasting his possessions. So he called him in and asked him, 'What is this I hear about you? Give an account of your management"…

Luke 16:1-2 New International Version

Principle – Churches that rely on spreadsheets and are content with presenting "summary" reports of "highlights" may end up getting burned.

In recent years, especially in the realm of politics, a new definition of the word spin has emerged. No longer does spin simply mean to rotate on an axis. It can also be defined as communicating a message in such a manner to influence the hearers' interpretation so that they will react in a desired manner. Hence, politicians often "spin" news to work to their best advantage (i.e. getting re-elected). But, politicians aren't the only ones guilty of this. If we are honest, most of us will admit that from early childhood on, when faced with giving difficult answers, we will try to answer in a way that is most favorable to our own situation. I think it is human nature to do so.

Several years ago a movie was made that is a good illustration of the art of "spinning." More importantly, the movie also teaches that the continued practice of spinning often makes things worse, not better. In "While You Were Sleeping," Sandra Bullock plays a young single woman named Lucy working as a ticket taker for the Chicago Transit Authority, Chicago's public transportation system. Lucy, who has no family, sits in a lonely ticket booth watching the people, and her life, go by. Day after day she takes tokens from the passengers wishing she could be a passenger herself, but not on the "L." In her day dreams, she falls in love with a handsome young professional named Peter that passes through her gate each morning. She fantasizes that this "Prince Charming" will marry her and take her on a honeymoon to Florence, Italy.

On Christmas Day Lucy's "Prince Charming" comes by, drops off a token and does something new. He speaks a few words to her, taking Lucy's breath away. Her eyes riveted to him, she follows his path to the platform where he is immediately mugged and thrown onto the tracks. Lucy rushes to him and moves him from the tracks just before a train barrels by. Unfortunately, he has been knocked unconscious. Lucy follows as he is taken to the hospital but is not allowed to enter because she is not "family."

As he is wheeled into a room, knowing that she probably would not be this close to him again, she mutters under her breath that she was going to marry him. A nurse standing nearby, hears Lucy's wishful thinking and mistakenly believes she is the young man's fiancée. The nurse escorts Lucy into the hospital room just before the victim's family arrives and promptly introduces Lucy to the family as their son's fiancée. This is where Lucy's "spin" begins.

First, rather than immediately clearing things up, she remains silent. While the family embraces her because she had saved Peter, she starts a feeble attempt to tell the truth. But, she decides to say nothing because she fears the truth could cause Peter's grandmother to have a heart attack. In an effort to spare the family from pain, Lucy commits herself to living a ruse, fully intending to disclose the truth at the earliest possible time. So, the spin continues...

In her second "spin" Lucy bends the truth a little bit. The family, curious about the future daughter-in-law they have never met, naturally has many questions. They are interested to find out how the two met and what was it about him she liked. Lucy, thinking on her crush on Peter, simply says that they "saw each other" and "it was his smile." Technically, the statements were not lies, but they really didn't answer the parents' questions and Lucy knew it. In an apparent attempt to work off some of her guilt, Lucy goes to Peter's room and apologizes to the comatose man. She falls asleep and accidentally spends the night in Peter's hospital room where the family finds her the next morning. This is where the third spin takes place.

The ruse is elevated to a new level when she accepts an invitation to come to the family's Christmas celebration. She is forced to stand in the family picture, receives a present and meets the rest of the family, including Peter's brother Jack. Because Jack is skeptical she is forced to repeat her first three spins including a new round of questions answered with half-truths. Although Jack eventually comes to believe her, not everyone does.

Peter's godfather figures out the fraud but this does not end the charade. Saul, the godfather, convinces her to continue the ruse telling her that the family hasn't been this happy in years and he wants them to be brought down gently. Saul convinces Lucy to continue the spin by becoming a willing participant in a deception "for the good of the family."

Her next reason for deception, while unrealistic, makes for a good movie; she falls in love with the brother! She continues to go along with the ruse, not only for the well being of the family, she now has a vested interest in keeping things going. If she were to confess, she would lose any chance at Jack and the family she suddenly has found. Telling the truth now would rob this lonely person of her newly found family.

Unfortunately, when telling the whole truth is put on hold, events can spin out of control. Unable to confess because she can't bring herself to hurt anyone (including herself now), Lucy eventually finds herself standing at the altar of the hospital's chapel, about to marry a man she knows only in her day-dreams, witnessed by the man she had come to love, and a family, something she had never really had. What a mess… it was past time for the spin to stop. She confessed to the whole thing. I'm going to stop right there because I don't want to spoil the ending for those who have not seen the film. Most importantly I'm stopping because I hope I have made my point. Churches sometimes play the role of Lucy.

Living like Lucy...

When it comes to preparing financial statements some churches behave in a similar nature. In order to tell their whole story a church should prepare and distribute a balance sheet, income statement/budget report and a designated/restricted funds schedule.[1] For a variety of reasons, like Lucy, some churches decide to not tell the whole truth by providing a full set of financial statements. Instead they are tempted, like Lucy, to keep a few things from the family. In many cases the reasons for doing so are good; other times not so much. Slowly but surely the goal of the church's financial reporting system will shift.

---

[1]These are generic terms; Generally Accepted Accounting Principles terms for Balance Sheet and Income statement are Statement of Financial Position and Statement of Activities, respectively.

The goal of a set of church financial statements is to fully inform the congregation of the church's economic health. What kind of assets does it own? How much money is in the bank? Is any of the cash restricted to certain uses? Is the church meeting its budget? Are the ministries of the church being accomplished? A full set of financial statements will go a long way in answering these questions.

Often the goal shifts and the purpose of the financial reports becomes to "spin" the results to accomplish one of two things; make everyone happy, or at least content or cover up bad behavior. One of the ways churches produce spin documents is by using spread sheets or summary presentations of financial activities. For a variety of reasons, some churches go overboard in their dependence on these types of reports. Many don't want to face endless questioning by certain deacons or finance team members who have a tendency to "micro-manage."

Others are simply fearful of telling bad news. With a summary, the bad things can be omitted and with "highlights" they can "spin" the situation. The goal is to provide a "soft landing" by making things sound a little better than they really are. Unfortunately, following this practice often does not result in a happy ending. There are two possible worst case scenarios.

It is possible to have two "worst" case scenarios...

If economic factors continue to deteriorate, a day of reckoning is certain to come. And when it does, it will be painful. With the exception of birthday parties, no one likes surprises. Church members, who have been going about their ministry thinking all is safe and secure will often over-react when out of the blue comes a warning: "things aren't so good right now." First comes shock, then anger, then retribution.

The *worst*, worst case scenario is that this type of financial reporting mechanism is a very effective smoke-screen for an embezzler. If a person bent on taking from the church is in control of the formats and types of reports the church sees, it may be open season on the church's assets. The embezzler will be sure to report to the church what the church wants to be told, but will have much more leverage in covering their tracks.

For example, electronic spreadsheets are powerful and effective tools that can be used to enhance a church's financial analysis. However, they have one huge problem. They are *too* user friendly. Cells can be changed at will and the information presented is totally at the mercy of the report preparer's intelligence and *integrity*. The double-entry accounting system was invented for a purpose; to insure that one hundred percent of the activity of an entity is accounted for and reported.

A firm foundation...

The foundation of a fraud-proof organization is the establishing of a strong accounting and financial reporting system. At least four key characteristics must be present in order for the church's accounting and reporting system to be effective in discouraging fraud and mis-management. First, it must be *accurate*. The numbers must be correct and reliable. In order to make effective decisions, the information provided the decision makers must be dependable. The statements must also be *timely*. Accounting information is a very perishable product; the longer it takes to produce the less value it holds for the readers. The information must also be relevant. And, most importantly, the reports must be complete. To meet these four criteria the church should consider taking a few well defined steps.

First, the church should *follow a budget*. Every church needs to know what "normal" is. It can prove very difficult to determine if theft is taking place if a church does not have any idea of what its financial expectations are. The budget should be adopted by the church's normal governance procedures and loaded into its accounting soft-ware. Budget results should be monitored and variations between budget and actual regularly examined. One word of warning: a practice frequently used by churches is to allow overspending in line-item accounts as long as total department expenditures remain within bud-get parameters for that department. This may not be the best practice. A budget is simply a tool and if a line-item is not sufficient, the budget should be amended by the appropriate leaders of the church. This preserves the concept of "normal" for each department. Much mayhem can take place within a single department budget!

The second step is to establish a *formal reporting system*. A formal reporting system should start with a well-defined chart of accounts. The chart of accounts should be a reflection of the budget; otherwise it will be very difficult to determine if the church is on the right financial course. In fact, best practices dictate that the general ledger should *exactly* reflect the budget adopted by the church.

Finally, the financial reports should be prepared and distributed regularly and on a timely basis. This is best accomplished by setting a due date to be met each and every month, the most common example being a monthly finance team or committee meeting. Tardy financial reporting by itself is not proof of fraudulent behavior and usually is the result of staff inexperience or incompetence. Yet, it is not a coincidence that in many church embezzlement cases, the absence of financial reports was a part of the problem.

Finally, the financial statements presented should have *full disclosure* as one of its goals. This means that the church should prepare and present a balance sheet, an income statement and a restricted fund activity statement at a minimum. A full set of financial reports can be an effective tool to monitor not only a church's activities but also its assets to provide protection against fraud. The following is an examination of how each statement, if used to its fullest, can help resist fraud.

The Balance Sheet (Statement of Financial Position)

The balance sheet reflects what the church owns, what it owes to others and its net worth (net assets). It also reflects restrictions placed on its assets by donors. One form of fraud prevention is to carefully read the balance sheet looking for changes (or the lack of changes) in various accounts. The following are a few questions that can be used to look for abnormalities. Each question is followed by a fraud technique that might go undetected if a church does not produce and use an accurate financial statement.

- Does the balance sheet include **all** of the bank accounts the church maintains? Is the monthly balance sheet being closely read to determine the presence of unusual swings in account balances, particularly involving non-operating accounts?

  ¤ Dormant accounts are a fraudster's best friend. If a church never looks at a balance sheet, disbursements out of these accounts probably will not be detected. Also, offerings could be diverted to these bank accounts that no one is aware of, followed by a transfer to the perpetrator's account.

- If the church has investment accounts, are they being recorded in the balance sheet? Are changes in asset value being reflected on a monthly basis?

  ¤ Churches seldom **"budget"** for interest and dividend income. If no balance sheet is issued the earnings from these accounts can easily be diverted.

- Are loan balances maintained on a regular basis? Are principal reductions recorded when made and reflected in the financial statements?

  ¤ In some cases, the first indication of fraud is the appearance of delinquency notices from a lender. An over-ambitious thief may have taken so much that there were insufficient resources to pay the loan payments. Because no one was looking at a balance sheet, there was no way to determine the situation until it was too late.

The Budget Report (Statement of Activities)

The statement of activities, usually called the budget report, reflects the income received and expenses paid by a church. In most cases, the church's activities are reported alongside the budget adopted by the church at the beginning of its fiscal year. Questions to ask are:

- *If budget to actual variances exist, what are they telling us?*

    ¤ *Budget variances can simply be the result of economic or attendance/giving factors. But, they can also be the result of bad behavior, another reason why variances should be examined line-by-line, not by department totals.*

- *How do revenues and expenses compare on a year-to-year, and period-to-period basis?*

    ¤ *Like budget variations, period variances can be the result of innocent factors. But, they can also be reflective of another change; a change in personnel.*

- *Has there been a change in expenses as a percentage of revenues?*

    ¤ *In aggressive cases, fraud can be significant enough to impact these percentage relationships.*

Restricted Fund Activity

For several reasons, particular attention should be given to restricted gifts. The most important reason is that by accepting a restricted gift, a church assumes fiduciary responsibility for the gift. Misspending restricted funds can result in severe legal implications. And occasionally, restricted gifts will sit idle for extended periods of time. These funds may prove to be irresistible to a thief. To avoid losing these types of funds a church should be intimately aware of what restricted funds are on hand and how they are being used. A monthly statement detailing beginning balances of each restricted fund, restricted gifts received, funds used and ending balances should be presented.

> • *How many restricted gifts do we maintain? Who established them? Are we using the money as directed? Do we have any accounts that appear to be dormant?*
>
> ¤ *The challenge a fraudster may have, particularly in regard to cash disbursement scams, is where to code or classify the phony expense. A popular place is a dormant or seldom used account.*

Recent headlines...

THE FINANCIAL REPORTS ONE CHURCH BUSINESS ADMINIS-
TRATOR PRESENTED TO HIS FINANCE COMMITTEE INCLUDED
A SIMPLE BUDGET REPORT AND A ONE-PAGE REPORT LIST-
ING THE CASH BALANCES IN THE CHURCH'S OPERATING,
SAVINGS, AND PAYROLL ACCOUNTS. WHEN HE DISCOVERED
THE EXISTENCE OF A LONG-FORGOTTEN AND DORMANT
BANK ACCOUNT HE BEGAN A PROCESS OF TRANSFERRING
SMALL AMOUNTS OF CASH FROM THE OTHER CHURCH BANK
ACCOUNTS. WITH A FORGED SIGNATURE CARD HE WAS
ABLE TO MAKE TRANSFERS FROM THIS ACCOUNT TO HIS
PERSONAL ACCOUNT. THE PRACTICE WENT ON FOR YEARS,
UNTIL A NEW FINANCE COMMITTEE MEMBER INSISTED ON
BEING PRESENTED WITH A BALANCE SHEET AS WELL AS THE
BUDGET REPORT.

ANOTHER CHURCH HAD A COMPREHENSIVE CHURCH-BASED
COMPUTER DATA MANAGEMENT SYSTEM. HOWEVER, THE
FINANCE COMMITTEE DID NOT CARE ABOUT A BALANCE
SHEET, PREFERRING ONLY A BUDGET REPORT. THE BUSINESS
ADMINISTRATOR, DISGRUNTLED AT THE FAILURE OF THE
CHURCH TO GIVE HIM A "WELL-DESERVED" RAISE, PRO-
CEEDED TO TAKE REGULAR "PERSONAL DRAWS" OUT OF THE
CHURCH'S BUILDING ACCOUNT. THE EXPENDITURES WERE
CLASSIFIED AGAINST THE CHURCH'S UNRESTRICTED NET
ASSET GENERAL LEDGER ACCOUNT. BECAUSE THE FINANCE
TEAM NEVER BOTHERED TO ASK FOR A BALANCE SHEET, THE
"RAISES" WERE NOT CAUGHT UNTIL THE BUSINESS ADMINIS-
TRATOR HAD MOVED ON TO ANOTHER JOB.

*If only these churches had...insisted on the inclusion
of a balance sheet with its monthly finance reports*

A CHURCH BOOKKEEPER PREPARED AN EXHAUSTIVE SET OF EXCEL SPREADSHEET REPORTS INCLUDING AN INCOME STATEMENT, CASH RECONCILIATION STATEMENTS AND A LISTING OF CHECKS WRITTEN DURING THE MONTH. FOR A PERIOD OF SEVERAL YEARS THE BOOKKEEPER REGULARLY PAID CAR PAYMENTS AND PERSONAL CREDIT CARD BILLS OUT OF CHURCH FUNDS. THE EXPENDITURES WERE BURIED IN THE REPAIRS AND MAINTENANCE LINE ITEM AND THE PAYEE WAS CHANGED ON THE CASH DISBURSEMENT LIST. THE BOOKKEEPER WAS NOT CAUGHT UNTIL THE CHURCH'S BANK CALLED TO INQUIRE WHY THE PAYMENTS WERE LATE. UNFORTUNATELY, THEY CALLED WHEN THE BOOKKEEPER WAS ON VACATION!

If only this church had relied on fully-integrated church financial software for accounting and reporting instead of electronic spread-sheets

Five point fraud prevention test...

- Has your church adopted and does it operate under the guidance of a formally approved annual budget?

- Is your finance committee presented with a complete set of financial statements including a balance sheet, income statement/budget report and a schedule of restricted funds activity?

- Are budget versus actual variances analyzed?

- Are your church's financial statements presented on a regular basis (monthly is preferred) and within a reasonable time after month-end?

- Are balance sheet accounts (cash, investments, notes payable, etc.) adjusted monthly and presented up-to-date in the church's financial statements?

Chapter 7

Are You Playing By the Rules?

*"Show me a denarius. Whose portrait and inscription are on it?" "Caesar's," they replied.
He said to them, "Then give to Caesar what is Caesar's, and to God what is God's."*

Luke 20:24-25, New International Version

Principle – Even though non-compliance with IRS rules does not necessarily constitute fraud, it can be an early warning signal that something is not right.

I'm not very fond of rules. Perhaps it is because, had it been possible back in the day, I would have been diagnosed as ADHD. I am antsy. I have got to be moving around and can't sit still for very long. I do not like things that hem me in…like rules!

Or maybe it's the era I grew up in – the sixties when the badge of honor was to rebel against anything and everything. In college we were challenged by many of our professors to question the "establishment" and its rules.

More than likely however, the real reason for my distrust of rules goes back to being raised by parents serious about their religion. The church I was raised in was extremely conservative. Included with this conservatism was a multitude of rules that I took great pleasure in breaking.

When I began working on this chapter I was immediately faced with a dilemma. How could I, a noted rule breaker according to many Sunday School teachers, write a chapter about "Playing by the Rules"? To help overcome this challenge I decided to do some research and consulted a dictionary. There was no shortage of definitions for the word "rule" and there seemed to be an equal division between nouns and verbs. I like the definitions of the nouns best; they were softer.

As a noun the word rule can mean "an established standard or habit of behavior[1]." That sounds reasonable enough. The noun was also defined as "an authoritative direction for conduct or procedure[2]." I'm not too wild about the word authoritative but on balance I can live with this; it's firm, but fair.

But the definitions of the verbs brought back childhood memories that even to this day send chills down my spine. "To exercise control over," "to dominate by powerful influence," and "to keep within proper limits…"[3] Boy! Does that describe some of the rules we used to face? Now, many years later, I actually look back with fondness on the things we did. In fact, many of the rules were downright funny. Let me share a few.

First of all, church was serious business and there was no better reflection of devotion than simply "being there."
A child whose parents taught Sunday School at our church started at eight o'clock every Sunday morning by helping get the rooms ready. That was just the beginning of a very, very, very long day. Sunday School started around nine and was followed by the worship service that stretched me almost to the starvation point. After church, came about two hours of rest before heading back for phase two; youth choir practice, evening worship service and Baptist Training Union the "boot camp for Baptists." The day finally ended when we arrived home around eight just in time to see Bonanza but not in time to see the Beatles on Ed Sullivan.

---

[1] The American Heritage Dictionary of the English Language; Houghton Mifflin Company; Boston
[2] Ibid.
[3] Ibid.

Given how often we were required to be at church, this next rule was next to impossible for young boys to live by. "No running in the halls!" What cruelty! You keep a group of ten year old boys cooped up all day and then actually expect them to walk quietly in the halls? Because of the need to vent pent up energy this was no doubt the most-defied rule of them all. It was so prevalent, that the adults always added a clause to the rule to be sure we knew how serious an offense running the halls was. "In the Lord's house..." It was hard enough to just obey our elders, but to drag God into it seemed a bit unfair.

As we grew into our teen years, running in the halls was replaced by other prohibitions, the most famous of which was drinking. Abstinence programs in those days had nothing to do with sex, they were all directed toward alcohol. Our church also had a quite extensive list of do's and don'ts, weighted heavily on the don't side. Other things we were not allowed to do were dancing, playing cards, going swimming on Sunday, chewing gum in church, etc., etc., etc.

Finally, there is one rule, which if it teaches nothing else, teaches the importance of exercising care in labeling your rules. I grew up and still live in Texas. In the summer it gets extremely hot, so back in my childhood, when air conditioning was not as common, swimming was extremely popular. At church events held in the summer, swimming was a staple. And it was fun. Except for one rule. Boys could never be in the pool at the same time as the girls. Church leaders gave co-ed swimming the unfortunate label of "mixed bathing." It was always fun to see the looks on the faces of visiting Methodists, or Presbyterians when they were told we would tolerate no "mixed bathing"!

I have poked some fun at these rules but actually I look back fondly at the things my parents and their fellow church members imposed on us. The fact of the matter is that they imposed these rules in the spirit of doing what they thought was best for us. And, with the exception of dancing and swimming, all of these rules make a good point about the spiritual life.

For example:

- *Being at church all day Sunday emphasized the importance of the Sabbath.*

- *Not being allowed to run in the church halls was intended to teach us reverence.*

- *Drinking: that one is obvious.*

- *When our parents came of age, card games were usually played in "less than honorable" places. They knew that bringing cards into a church setting didn't harm the players but it could tarnish God's name.*

There is one other thing about rules that should not be overlooked; they usually do not just happen on their own. Rules usually come into existence after someone has done something wrong. They exist to remind us that the paths we walk can be dangerous. Willful disregard can be an indicator of serious problems. We all complain about the IRS and the Tax Code it enforces. But they only exist because people sometimes have difficulty doing the right thing.

What does this have to do with church fraud?

Although technically tax-exempt, churches are hardly "tax-free." First, churches do pay some taxes. For example, churches with non-ministerial employees pay payroll taxes, churches collect and remit sales taxes, and in local jurisdictions many churches pay real estate taxes. And even though they are exempt from federal income taxes, churches must comply with a myriad of rules and regulations in order to remain exempt.

It must be pointed out that having "IRS problems" does not necessarily mean illicit behavior has taken place. But, since many of the IRS rules were created in reaction to someone's bad behavior, the possibility of fraud is definitely something that should cross one's mind. Tax compliance should be an integral part of all churches' systems of fraud prevention.

Compliance with the Internal Revenue Code is much more than simply abiding by the law of the land, although that is very important. Compliance is also a form of exercising a "best practices" approach to management. It also serves as another form of accountability because being accountable to the government aids the church in being accountable to the congregation. Also, by exercising strong compliance with the tax laws, many portals by which fraudsters can gain entry to a church are tightly shut.

Even seemingly small instances of non-compliance can be indicators of bad behavior. For example, it is not unusual for a new church business administrator to discover a stack of penalty notices from the IRS for late deposits. Usually, the presence of the penalty notices is attributed to the complexity of the IRS rules or the inability of the church to hire qualified administrative staff.

However, there could be a more sinister reason for the notices and unfortunately, this scenario is usually not considered until extreme damage has been done. Consider these facts. Most churches operate out of budgets in order to keep track of their spending. Proficient thieves know this and realize that to get away with the money they must overcome a challenge. How do they both drain the church bank account and hide the evidence at the same time? This dilemma results in some very interesting juggling acts. To overcome this challenge, embezzlers tend to hide in the "tall weeds," which in a church budget would be equivalent to the larger numbers.

The normal technique is to take from vendors whose squeal is the softest *or* least frequent. That is what makes tax deposits attractive. First, because salary is usually a church's largest expense, tax deposits will be large, too. And even though ultimately the IRS has the loudest squeal, its squeal can be timed. A bookkeeper facing some type of personal crisis may be tempted to "borrow" from the church by not making the tax deposits and using the funds to take care of their crisis. Because their "intention" is always to pay the money back, as long as the money is restored before the end of the quarter, the only harm done will be the late payment penalties. Unfortunately, the story seldom ends there because the money cannot be paid back. The church's and employees' money is gone and the damage continues with additional penalties.

All of it could have been avoided if the first penalty notice had been investigated. A simple investigation would have revealed that the penalty occurred because the deposit was not made when the church's books said it was. Playing by the IRS rules is another brick in the wall of fraud protection.

A shared goal...

There is a great deal of discussion, often heated, about the separation of church and state. But, there is unity in one area. Although they have two different motivations, when it comes to accountability, government and church share the same goal – a church's money should be used to benefit many, not just a few.

The church's motivation is spiritual. The money belongs to God, not to individuals and it should be protected. This is called "stewardship." Taking the funds for personal use is not simply against the law, it is sin. The government's motivation is based on the simple principle that the reason non-profit organizations exist is to help the public at large. Individuals are not to benefit from their involvement with a charity and transfers of an organization's funds to individuals can only take one of two forms: reasonable salaries or assistance to individuals in some type of need. Any other transfer of funds to an individual is looked upon with a great deal of skepticism. Churches should agree with this sentiment, because, in short, most other cases constitute some type of theft.

It all sounds so simple. But it's not. And the complexity explains why the Internal Revenue Code has so many rules. To show how this dovetails with fraud concerns we are going to look at two of the IRS's major concerns.

"The laborer is worthy of his hire..." [4]

The tax law recognizes the need for churches and other charities to adequately pay their workers. In fact, I have a suspicion that the IRS is a little more generous than some church personnel committees! But, the IRS qualifies its generosity by defining adequate salary as "reasonable compensation." Needless to say, there is a great deal of disagreement over what "reasonable" means. On one hand, it's not a good practice to pay ministers at subsistence levels. On the other hand, a senior pastor should not be able to dip into the church bank account at will. There needs to be balance. The Code attempts to deliver this balance by establishing a three point process to be used in setting salaries. If a church adopts this they will take a good step towards compliance with the rules. A bi-product is that they will also take a good step forward in building their anti-fraud wall of protection.

The three steps are:

- *Requiring the compensation arrangements for all staff, but most importantly senior staff, be set by an independent compensation or personnel committee.*

- *Conduct a salary comparison survey to determine if the compensation is in line with the market.*

- *Document the decisions made in formal, contemporaneous minutes or resolutions.*

In addition to the setting of basic compensation determination, the church must also comply with the rules regarding all of the "perks" given to its employees. A good rule of thumb to remember: "there is no free lunch." The government has laid down guidelines for virtually every imaginable way an individual can receive benefits from

[4] 1 Timothy 5:18; American Standard Version,

employers. In order to take care of their pastors, churches will often provide medical benefits, tuition assistance, child care services and home maintenance to name just a few. If that is the case, the church must be sure that it is administering the benefits under an IRS compliant plan document. And, if a new minister asks for something outside of the usual, stand your ground when you hear a familiar refrain: "At my last church they did this and the IRS never said a thing…"

Payments to individuals...

When our firm audits a church, one of the steps we take is to analyze the check register. With spreadsheet software this has become extremely easy. The most useful technique is to sort the data by vendor. In just a few minutes, preliminary assessments can be made of what is going on, financially at least, at the church. The disbursements focused on are payments to individuals, because in addition to being important to the IRS, excessive payments to individuals may indicate a breakdown in security.

It's not an option...

One frequent noncompliance issue is the payment of individuals as independent contractors. There is a widespread misconception that a person receiving payment can "elect" to be treated as a contractor. This is not true as the tax law has a test to be followed to determine status of the recipient. And the status is determined by how much control the payer has over the recipient, not the wishes of the recipient. Paying individuals outside of the payroll process is so crucial, churches should exercise significant control over the process by keeping a record of all contractors, securing tax identification numbers from all contractors and issuing year-end 1099 forms.

Benevolence...

Because in most cases no services were given by the recipient, 1099s are not issued to benevolence recipients. That lack of accountability to the government makes benevolence funds a favorite target of perpetrators of fraud. Often, they will bury their illicit "assistance payments" in the benevolence accounts. Even though no formal, routine reporting is required, churches should keep in mind that they must be able to prove quickly and easily how each disbursement it makes furthers its exempt purpose. To stay in compliance, and close down fraud portals a church's benevolence activity should be governed by a written benevolence policy that establishes unequivocal procedures for assistance payments.

Pastors aren't always discretionary...

A close cousin to benevolence funds is the establishment of an account allowing a pastor to make anonymous assistance payments. This arrangement is most commonly referred to as a "pastors discretionary fund." While this practice has its merits, a few things should be kept in mind. First the tax consequences must be considered. If the pastor can use *any* of the proceeds for personal needs the entire amount is taxable. Churches should take care to keep their pastors from stumbling into a problem. Second, we all need to be accountable, even the senior leadership. Anonymity may be important but it is not as important as the credibility of the pastor. At a minimum, the payment decision should be shared with one other trusted church official. Finally, some of the more spectacular fraud cases have involved discretionary funds. This is the kind of publicity no church needs or wants.

Plastic...

The newest kids on the fraud block are those who misuse credit cards and online shopping. Many churches have not updated their procurement processes to include this new way of buying. As a result, an individual will assume they can purchase at will. If the processes are not updated trouble is often not far behind.

Recent headlines...

"Sounds reasonable to me!"

PASTOR BOB PLANTED HIS CHURCH IN A GROWING SUBURB OF THE CITY. THE CHURCH HAS GROWN RAPIDLY, BOTH IN MEMBERS AND BUDGET DOLLARS. NEVER ONE TO TRUST COMMITTEES, PASTOR BOB'S CHURCH GOVERNANCE CONSISTS OF A BOARD OF ELDERS INCLUDING HIMSELF, HIS WIFE, HIS TWO SONS AND HIS SON-IN-LAW. DURING

THE PAST YEAR PASTOR BOB "DREW" A MONTHLY SALARY OF $25,000. IN ADDITION, ON CHRISTMAS EVE HE PAID HIMSELF A HOUSING ALLOWANCE OF $50,000 AND GAVE A CHRISTMAS GIFT TO HIS GRANDSON BY PAYING COLLEGE TUITION FOR THE COMING SEMESTER. THE CHURCH ALSO PAID PASTOR BOB $10,000 IN MEDICAL EXPENSE REIMBURSEMENTS BUT DID NOT HAVE A PLAN OR REQUIRE HIM TO DOCUMENT THE EXPENSES. IN THE COURSE OF A "ROUTINE" IRS PAYROLL TAX AUDIT TRIGGERED BY LATE TAX DEPOSITS, THE CONGREGATION WAS SHOCKED TO LEARN THAT THE PASTOR, WHO HAD BEEN CALLING THEM TO GIVE SACRIFICIALLY, WAS BEING PAID IN EXCESS OF $400,000!

If only this church had an independent compensation committee familiar with IRS tax rules.

What's in YOUR wallet???

PASTOR BILL WAS ACTIVE IN THE COMMUNITY, BEING A MEMBER OF SEVERAL COUNTRY CLUBS AS WELL AS SERVING ON CIVIC BOARDS. BECAUSE HE FELT THIS WAS PART OF HIS OUTREACH, HE WAS REIMBURSED MORE THAN $500 EACH MONTH FOR HIS OUT-OF-POCKET EXPENSES. IN ADDITION, HE CARRIED A CREDIT CARD IN THE CHURCH'S NAME WHICH HE WOULD USE FOR "BIG" OCCASIONS. THE PASTOR WAS NOT REQUIRED TO PROVIDE ANY DOCUMENTATION TO ESTABLISH THE BUSINESS PURPOSE OF THE EXPENDITURES. UNFORTUNATELY, THE PASTOR UNDERWENT AN IRS AUDIT DURING WHICH THE EXPENSES WERE UNCOVERED. NOT ONLY WAS THE CHURCH SUBJECTED TO INTERMEDIATE SANCTION PENALTIES, IT ALSO SUFFERED THE INDIGNITY OF LEARNING THAT MORE THAN $20,000 IN HIGHLY QUESTIONABLE PERSONAL EXPENSES WERE PAID ON THE CHURCH CREDIT CARD.

Now that's what I call money laundering...

MATT, THE YOUTH GUY, NOTICED THAT THE CHURCH REGU-
LARLY REIMBURSED EXPENSES INCURRED ON ITS BEHALF
BUT HAD NO REQUIREMENTS TO PROVIDE DOCUMENTATION.
HE ALSO NOTED THAT NO ONE LOOKED VERY CLOSELY AT
THE FEW RECEIPTS THAT WERE TURNED IN. AS A RESULT,
HE BEGAN TO TURN IN ANY RECEIPTS THAT COULD BE
REMOTELY CONNECTED TO HIS WORK. EVENTUALLY, HE EVEN
CAST OFF THAT RESTRAINT AND TURNED IN PERSONAL
ITEMS BECAUSE, IN HIS MIND, "THE CHURCH WASN'T
PAYING HIM A LIVING WAGE ANYWAY." EVENTUALLY, AT
THE URGING OF AN IRATE FINANCE COMMITTEE MEMBER, A
REVIEW OF HIS REIMBURSEMENTS WAS CONDUCTED. MATT,
THE YOUTH GUY, HAD BEEN REIMBURSED MORE THAN
$5,000 IN ONE YEAR. INCLUDED IN THE REIMBURSEMENTS
WAS A NEW WASHING MACHINE FOR HIS APARTMENT. HE
JUSTIFIED THE PURCHASE BECAUSE HE FREQUENTLY TOOK
THE YOUTH GROUP "PAINT-BALLING."

*If only these churches had adopted and lived by an
accountable reimbursement plan governing expense
reimbursements. A written credit card policy governing the use of church issued credit cards would have
been useful as well.*

Benevolence

MRS. SMITH, A LONG-TIME MEMBER OF COMMUNITY
CHURCH, GAVE $50,000 TO THE CHURCH TO ESTABLISH A
FUND TO HELP HOMELESS AND OUT-OF-WORK INDIVIDUALS.
IN ADDITION, THE CHURCH CONTRIBUTED $10,000 FROM ITS
BUDGET TO THE FUND AND ENCOURAGED MEMBERS TO GIVE
AS WELL. BECAUSE OF HER "GENEROSITY," THE CHURCH

APPOINTED MRS. SMITH TO BE THE SOLE ADMINISTRA-TOR OF THE FUND. ALSO, BECAUSE OF HER MANY YEARS OF DEVOTION TO THE CHURCH, THEY SAW NO NEED TO ESTABLISH A BENEVOLENCE FUND POLICY. AT THE END OF THE FIRST YEAR OF THE FUND'S EXISTENCE, THE CHURCH'S AUDITORS FOUND SOME INTERESTING DISBURSEMENTS. IN ADDITION TO THE SMALL RENT ASSISTANCE CHECKS FOR INDIVIDUALS TRULY IN NEED, WERE A $25,000 TUITION PAYMENTS FOR ONE "JOHNNY SMITH" AND MORTGAGE PAYMENTS FOR MRS. SMITH'S OUT-OF-WORK DAUGHTER TOTALING $15,000.

If only this church had written a benevolence policy to administer the distribution of assistance payments and appointed a team to evaluate benevolence candidates and assess needs.

Five point fraud prevention test...

- *Does your church address "reasonable compensation" issues by:*

    - ¤ *Establishing an independent compensation committee?*

    - ¤ *Basing compensation on comparative market data?*

    - ¤ *Documenting adequately compensation issues?*

- *Does your church have processes in place that give assurance that all fringe benefits provided staff are governed by an IRS or Department of Labor compliant plan?*

- *If your church reimburses its employees for business expenses, has it adopted an IRS compliant accountable reimbursement plan?*

- *Has your church implemented a "contractor" approval process to screen potential independent contractors which includes an application or approval form, background checks, obtaining tax identification numbers, and issuance of form 1099?*

- *Does your church use a committee or team approach to administering benevolence funds and is the team guided by a written, detailed assistance payment policy?*

Weeds in the Garden

Chapter 8

Do You Have Any Idea How Much Money You Make?

Bring the whole tithe into the storehouse, that there may be food in my house.

Malachi 3:10, New International Version

Principle – Churches that do not institute strong cash collection procedures (Seven days a week, not just Sundays) are likely to get "skimmed."

Anyone familiar with the Andy Griffith Show knows that Barney Fife had two big problems with secrets. First, when a secret was kept from him, Barney's curiosity absolutely killed him. On the other hand, once he was let in on a secret, he found it impossible to keep it to himself. Whether it was the mistaken belief that Andy and Helen were about to get married or the drinking habits of some of Mayberry's citizens, Barney couldn't keep it in. A secret to Barney was like money burning a hole in a teenage boy's pocket; it had to be shared.

In one episode, two Treasury Agents pay a visit to the courthouse and ask to see Sheriff Taylor. Because Andy is out on rounds Barney advises the agents that he can handle things. But to his consternation, the agents curtly tell him they will wait. Barney spends the next few minutes trying to wrestle the purpose of their visit from them, all to no avail. Making matters worse, when Andy finally returns, they ask to speak with the sheriff alone. Barney leaves in a huff, but tries his best to eavesdrop on their conversation through the mail drop.

After the meeting, Andy fills Barney in. The news is big and it must be kept quiet. "Tight Lips Barney," as he refers to himself, assures Andy that the secret is safe with him. A shipment of gold, on its way to Fort Knox, is coming though Mayberry. One armored car, with seven million dollars worth of gold bricks is going to pass right down Main Street and stop to refuel at Gomer Pyle's filling station.

Immediately, the excitable Barney Fife, blurts out, "This is big; the biggest thing in the history of Mayberry!" Andy reminds Barney they have only two roles in the gold transfer: Maintain absolute secrecy and anticipate every possible threat and guard against it.

However, the cat gets out of the bag! Barney immediately calls his "other girl friend" Juanita, informing her that they would have to cancel their date. Unfortunately, rather than making up a lame excuse, Barney tells her that something BIG is happening that requires his attention. She asks "Tight Lips Barney" what it could be, to which Barney replies she could never guess; then he foolishly lets her try. When she makes a bad guess, instead of saying she was cold; Barney says "gold"…

The secret is out and word spreads through Mayberry like a prairie fire. A carnival atmosphere engulfs the town and apparently all of its citizens gather on Main Street to "welcome" the truck. So many people arrive, that the truck cannot make it through the congestion. Eventually, Andy is able to clear enough of a path for the truck to make it on to the gas station for refueling and allow the agents time to take a short dinner break.

While this is taking place, Barney is posted inside the armored car and finds himself sitting among seven million dollars worth of gold, neatly packaged in cardboard boxes. Once again, his "need to know" gets the better of him and Barney decides to take a peek at a gold bar. After all, he has never seen one before. Barney makes a startling discovery. The boxes are not full of gold. They are full of sand!

Thinking there has been a heist, Barney begins to scream. But before he can make much of a ruckus, the agents cram him back in the truck and take off. Andy is surprised at the haste of their departure and the fate of his deputy. He follows in hot pursuit, catches the truck and with a drawn gun demands answers

Boy is he surprised! The agents grabbed Barney and took off because he was about to reveal their secret. The Mayberry truck was a decoy! The plan was to make people think the gold was in the Mayberry truck while the real delivery went another, super-secret route. The agents knew the gold truck would create such a stir that the real gold shipment would slip through Raleigh, undetected! There was never any emergency as far as the Feds were concerned; *they knew where their money was every step of the way.*

It is ok for a church to keep secrets...

The government agents did not want the route of their gold known. Nor did they want the actual amount known, so they went to great lengths to conceal the truth by developing a very cynical diversion. They took advantage of the fact that in small towns, secrets have a very short shelf life. It reminds me of a wall plaque I saw in a client's office located in a small town. "It's true there is not much to see in a small town; but what you hear sure makes up for it"!

The fact was, the government knew exactly how much gold was involved, which truck it was in and which route it was taking. Many churches would do well to imitate the government agents in this story. Actually, most churches are fairly efficient on Sundays. But the rest of the week? Many churches resemble Mayberry.

Speaking of Fort Knox...

When church fraud or embezzlement is mentioned most people immediately think of someone stealing from the offering plates. As a result, many, if not most churches do a pretty good job of protecting the Sunday offerings. In fact, many actually go overboard in tightly ratcheting down the money that comes into the church during worship services and Sunday School classes. Nevertheless, it is good to review some practices. Just like the agents passing through Mayberry, a church needs to know the whereabouts of its money *every step of the way*.

Let's split things up...

There is one cardinal rule that should govern the design of a church's cash collection procedures. A church should design its cash receipts system in such a way that its money is never in an unsecured position, even for the shortest periods of time. Put another way, a church's money should never be in the possession of one individual for any amount of time. As you will see in one of our case studies, just a few seconds can prove to be too long.

The main way this is accomplished is by integrating into the collection process something accountants call "segregation of duties." Simply put, this means splitting the work among as many people as possible so that one individual is not able to dominate the process. Here are a handful of steps that should be taken to accomplish this:

- *Cash collection, whether from the worship services, classrooms or kiosks should always involve at **least** two, preferably more participants.*

- *Offerings should be counted and recorded by count teams. The teams should consist of members who:*
    - ¤ *Serve rotating terms*
    - ¤ *Are not related to each other*
    - ¤ *Preferably are not members of the church staff*

- *If it is necessary to store offering overnight, the money should be kept in a safe that requires the participation of at least two individuals for access.*

- *The next phase of the process, transportation, should mirror the first phase. The deposit should be transported to the bank by at least two individuals if armored car service is too expensive.*

- *If at all possible, individuals responsible for general ledger and financial statement preparation should not participate in the counting and depositing of funds. Allowing these individuals to participate in counting weakens the integrity of the financial statements in that those doing the reporting are in essence reporting on themselves.*

- *Similarly, the tasks of maintaining church member contribution records should be separated from the counting and depositing of funds. Access to individual giving information should also be strictly limited. To enhance controls over contributions, many churches also perform periodic reconciliations between the total contributions reflected in the giving module with the actual amount of cash deposited. Investigating variances promptly sends a clear message to potential thieves that the church is watching things closely.*

Budgets...

Often, budgets are used for only one purpose in the church setting. And that is simply to determine if the church is going to have enough money to pay all of its bills. While this is probably the most important function of a budget, it is by no means the only one. Very few churches take the time to mine all of the treasure that their own budget records hold and the variety of benefits budgets can provide.

One such benefit, if a budget report is regularly read and analyzed, is that it can serve as an early detector of illicit behavior. Annual, quarterly, and monthly expectations help form baselines upon which judgments and assessments can be made. Budgets allow churches to target their expectations and if variations are examined on a regular basis, abnormalities can be spotted.

One word of advice is in order here. Most churches organize their budgets according to department areas like worship, pastoral, education, and missions. Occasionally, ministers are required to simply keep their total spending within the total department budget amount but are allowed to overspend, without review, individual line items. Although this practice may be more "efficient," it weakens the effectiveness of the budget both as a management tool and as a fraud prevention measure.

Don't be a Sunday's child...

When I was a teenager, there was a musical for Christian youth making the rounds of the bigger churches. The name of the musical escapes me but it contained one song titled "Sunday's Child." To the best of my memory one line went something like; "Sunday's Child, yes he's a Sunday's child, on Sundays he is quite a saint. But, Monday, Tuesday, Wednesday, Thursday, Friday and Saturday…a saint he ain't!" The point of the song was the need to live out our Christian faith seven days a week, not just making a pious show of ourselves on Sundays.

Thinking back on this song reminds me of the cash receipts practices of many churches. Sunday offerings are tightly controlled and many churches proudly broadcast their devotion to integrity of the process. But, Monday through Saturday? Anything goes! And, in most cases, we are not talking peanuts here. Many churches take in considerable sums of cash on weekdays. Three major types of cash flows are weekday drop-offs, special events (banquets, conference fees, etc.) and service fees such as tuition. The following is a discussion of each of these three types of revenues, the typical practices followed by many churches, the fraud risks involved, and a few best practices suggestions.

Weekday receipts...

No church has one hundred percent attendance and many church members, to their credit, do not feel right holding on to their gift until the next Sunday. As a result, they will make an effort to bring their offering envelope to the church during the week. This is not limited to offerings, however, as special event fees (conferences, banquets, etc.) and service charges (school tuition) also make their way to the church office during business hours.

Typical practices. Dropped-off money finds its way directly to the church accountant or bookkeeper and piles of cash will frequently accumulate on an overworked accountant's desk. The bookkeeper serves as a one-man teller team with the responsibility to count, record, and deposit the cash and enter transactions in the church's general ledger. Deposits are seldom made daily and as a result, cash is often left in unsecured locations overnight.

Fraud risks. At the lowest level, fraud can take place when cash is simply pocketed by anyone entering the business office. At the most significant level, an "ethically challenged" accountant can manip-ulate the records to reflect whatever he or she wants or needs them to say. For instance, because the bookkeeper is also the teller, a deposit can be made for less than was received and the dishonest employee may pocket the balance.

Best practices. The starting point for closing this weak spot is to assign cashier duties to an individual not involved in the account-ing and reporting process. Typically this is the church receptionist or office assistant. This individual would be given the responsibility for maintaining a log or receipt book to record receipt. After log-in, the funds are then turned over to the bookkeeping department for deposit and recording. (If confidentiality is an issue, the log can simply list the date, time and name of the individual dropping off the funds). Alternatively, some churches have a lock box or floor safe in which the funds are placed after recording in a cashier's log or receipt book. The box contents are emptied by the count team and included in the Sunday offering processes.

Special events...

All churches hold activities outside the normal activities of worship services, Sunday School, and prayer meetings. Some examples are banquets, camps, retreats, and conferences. In the vast majority of situations, these "special events" are funded by charging a fee or conducting a fund-raising activity. If these events are not managed properly, even in the best of cases, they will prove to be quite a headache. In the worst of cases, they may prove to be an irresistible invitation to commit fraud.

Typical practices. Often, because of the packed workloads of church paid staff, special events are managed completely by volunteers. Seldom, are any uniform cash procedures established by the church and each volunteer simply takes care of things as they see fit. Accordingly, the only cash register is a bank bag, and bill paying consists of simply taking money out of the bag. At the end of the event, the "net earnings" are turned over to the church business office. No accounting for the activity is required and no reconciliation of the revenues generated with the tickets or goods sold performed. Documentation of expenditures is often sketchy, at best.

Fraud risks. Several times I have performed Internet searches and come across a story like this. A church engages in a fund raising event that will last for a period of three months. In the first month much of the money will be raised but no expenses will be incurred resulting in "idle" cash. During this initial phase, the volunteer "treasurer" helps herself to several thousand dollars to do some home improving with the intention of paying it back before campaign expenses begin to roll in. Keep in mind that in the majority of non-profit organization fraud cases the money was "borrowed" not stolen. Unfortunately, the treasurer's husband lost his job and the money could not be paid back. The church loses, but it may never know it, due to its lack of control over the processes.

Best practices. If at all possible, all events being conducted in the church's name should be accounted for through the church office. Obviously, because of time limitations, this can prove to be very difficult. However, one way many churches are addressing special events is by turning to online giving/event fee software. This removes the necessity to have satellite cash collection points and provides some accounting and reporting features as well.

If this is not possible, time should be taken to develop and document special event administration procedures. In addition to cash collection and disbursement procedures, such a policy should require the preparation of a special events report. The report should be presented periodically, and include at a minimum the total number of goods or tickets sold, the total revenues generated and a listing and documentation of expenditures. Cash should be deposited at a minimum weekly!

Service Fees...

Some churches generate revenues that are the result of "business type" activities in which the church charges a fee in return for providing a service. The most common types of these sources of income are private school tuition, child care fees and professional counseling charges.

Typical practices. Many smaller churches maintain their accounting records primarily on the cash basis. Revenue is recognized when cash is received and expenses are recorded when the bills are paid. While this method is not in line with generally accepted accounting principles, it works well for most churches because of their "budget driven" natures. Unfortunately, when churches move into some type of business activity, the cash basis of accounting tends to move with them.

Using a private school as an example, it is not uncommon to find the following situations:

- *Revenues are recorded when tuition payments are received; payments may or may not be reflective of the academic year.*

- *No accounting is made for unearned revenues such as registration fees for the next term.*

- *Student accounts receivable is not managed.*

- *Expenses are only recognized when the bills are paid, which often translates when the money is available.*

Fraud risks. Schools can be a tricky accounting proposition because timing plays such a large part in the equation. This results in several weak spots;

- *Because registration and tuition deposits are frequently collected far in advance of the beginning of classes, many schools have significant "idle" cash. If these deposits are not managed and accounted for separately from tuition, fraudsters can easily raid them with little chance of detection.*

- *With no accounts receivable management, many churches have no way of knowing the total amount of uncollected accounts receivable or the individuals who are indebted to the church. It will also be impossible to identify nonperforming accounts. As a result, a cash-strapped bookkeeper may grant "scholarships" to his own children with no one suspecting a thing.*

- *Because the income and expense reports reflect cash activity, not economic activity, it can become difficult to establish baselines upon which to make comparisons. This makes it much easier for fraudulent expenses to be concealed.*

Best practices. Churches that enter into ongoing and substantial business-type activities should adopt the accrual basis of accounting, recognizing revenues when they are earned and expenses when they incurred. In addition, if credit is extended to customers, a business style accounts receivable system should be adopted.

Meanwhile, back in Mayberry...

Churches need to be like the Treasury Agents that sent their "gold" through Mayberry. They need to know intimately how the money flows through their church organizational structure. They need to never forget that people can get very excited about money. Congregations can get up in arms for far, far less than seven million dollars. Just like the agents, churches need to remember that the best way to insure that their money gets to its proper place is through a well-crafted plan. It does not happen by accident.

Recent headlines...

Talk about poor tone at the top...

TWO SENIOR MINISTERS WHO AUTHORITIES SAY STOLE THOUSANDS OF DOLLARS OF CASH FROM THEIR CHURCH'S OFFERING PLATES AND HID IT IN THE CHURCH CEILING WILL SOON BE GOING TO TRIAL. THE TWO PASTORS ARE ACCUSED OF BILKING THEIR CONGREGATION OF MORE THAN $850,000 DURING THE TIME IN WHICH THEY CAN BE CHARGED DUE TO THE STATUTE OF LIMITATIONS. INDEPENDENT AUDITORS ESTIMATE MORE THAN EIGHT MILLION DOLLARS WAS TAKEN OVER A PERIOD OF TWENTY YEARS. PROSECUTORS BELIEVE THE MEN TOOK CASH FROM THE OFFERING PLATES AND SPENT IT ON UPSCALE HOMES, GAMBLING TRIPS TO LAS VEGAS AND A RARE COIN COLLECTION.

If only this church had given its cash collection, recording and depositing responsibilities to a teller team with multiple, unrelated members, with rotating terms of service.

The Fall of the House of [this] Usher...

ACCORDING TO THE COUNTY DISTRICT ATTORNEY, A MAN SERVING AS AN USHER AT FIRST COMMUNITY FELLOWSHIP WILL BE CHARGED WITH THEFT. AFTER BECOMING SUSPICIOUS THAT THINGS WERE NOT RIGHT, THE CHURCH SET UP A SURVEILLANCE VIDEO THAT CAUGHT THE USHER REMOVING MONEY FROM THE OFFERING PLATES AFTER WORSHIP SERVICES. AUTHORITIES ESTIMATE MORE THAN EIGHT THOUSAND DOLLARS WAS STOLEN.

If only this church had established a policy requiring funds to be transferred to the count room by at least two individuals.

Don't be a stuffed shirt...

GRACE CHURCH HAS DECIDED TO NOT PRESS CHARGES AGAINST ONE OF ITS USHERS BECAUSE THE AMOUNT OF LOSS COULD NOT BE ADEQUATELY DOCUMENTED. JANE SMITH SERVED AS ONE OF THE BALCONY USHERS FOR THE CHURCH AND MADE IT A PRACTICE TO STUFF BILLS INTO HER BLOUSE WHILE MAKING HER WAY DOWN A FLIGHT OF STAIRS FROM THE BALCONY TO THE CHURCH FOYER. SHE WAS CAUGHT ONLY BECAUSE SHE INADVERTENTLY PICKED UP SOME COINS IN HER LAST ATTEMPT TO STEAL, WHICH MADE THEIR WAY THROUGH HER BLOUSE AND ONTO THE TILE FLOOR.

If only this church knew that money cannot be in anyone's sole custody for ANY amount of time, no matter how short.

Now let this be a lesson to you...

A FORMER TEACHER HAS BEEN ACCUSED OF STEALING MORE THAN $140,000 IN TUITION PAYMENTS FROM THE SCHOOL BY INSTRUCTING STUDENTS TO SEND PAYMENTS TO A POST OFFICE BOX HE HAD ESTABLISHED. BECAUSE NO ACCOUNTS RECEIVABLE RECORDS WERE MAINTAINED THE THEFTS WERE NOT DISCOVERED UNTIL A NEW ACCOUNTANT WAS HIRED WHO NOTICED IRREGULARITIES BETWEEN ENROLLMENT FIGURES AND REVENUES DEPOSITED.

If only this church/school had implemented a billing system and maintained individual student account information and activity.

Five point fraud prevention test...

- *Has your church examined its cash receipts processes and determined that from the time of collection to the time of deposit, cash is never, even for just a few minutes, in the custody of one individual?*

- *If your church stores cash overnight, is it kept in a safe that requires the participation of at least two individuals to gain access?*

- *Does your church have someone other than the book-keeper or accountant to serve as cashier?*

- *Does your church require full and timely reporting of special events managed by volunteers?*

- *Are Sunday offerings counted by a teller team made up of unrelated members who serve rotating terms?*

Weeds in the Garden

Chapter 9

Can't You Control Your Spending?

So he called ten of his servants and gave them ten minas. 'Put this money to work,' he said, 'until I come back.'

Luke 19:13,New International Version

Principle – Churches that do not watch over their expenditures with strong policies, procedures and controls are susceptible to disbursement fraud."

Most Americans are very concerned about their money. There is no better way to prove this than by performing a search on Amazon. By keying in "personal finance" or "personal spending" a listing of more than 35,000 titles will appear, some with some rather amusing titles. Interested readers can learn: "How to "Get a Grip on Your Money," "Ways You can "De-gunk Your Finances," and the art of "Pinching Dollars"! One is right up my alley; "The Idiot's Guide to Managing Money." But, my favorite is "Stop Me Because I Can't Stop Myself!"

It seems some would argue that not "everyone" is worried about their money, especially in regard to how to spend it wisely. This is really nothing new. Over one hundred and fifty years ago Charles Dickens created probably the most famous of all money managers: Ebenezer Scrooge: "A squeezing, wrenching, grasping, scraping, clutching, covetous, old sinner!" And, that is just the introduction. Dickens goes on to describe Ebenezer Scrooge as hard as flint but without the ability to produce generous fire. He was "secretive, self-contained and solitary as an oyster."[1]

Every judgment Scrooge made and every value he held dear was determined through the filter of commerce. Thrift and accumulation were the principles he lived by. And it affected his outlook on *everything*.

Take employee relations and fringe benefits for example. Scrooge employed an open door policy with his employees, but unfortunately not for the purpose of making himself accessible. Scrooge kept his office door wide open for the sole purpose of keeping his eye on his clerk, Bob Cratchett. Scrooge wanted to make sure he was getting his money's worth. When discussing the fringe benefits Scrooge provided his employees, the emphasis should always be on the first word: fringe. He only allowed his employee one small coal each day for warmth and to make sure he was not taken advantage of, the coal box was kept in Ebenezer's office. Scrooge's philosophy on vacation pay was quite simple; he equated an employee asking for time off with a pick-pocket.

The impact of Scrooge's miserable nature didn't stop at his office door. Scrooge had a general disdain for his fellow man. When the word generosity was mentioned, an involuntary frown would come over his face. Sadly, for the majority of his life, Scrooge resisted a relationship with his only living relative.

The result of this life of grasping, scraping and clutching was that Scrooge had money; but nothing else. He was a miserable, lonely and bitter rich man. Scrooge had difficulty managing money because he let his money manage him.

About eighteen hundred years before Charles Dickens told us about Ebenezer Scrooge, Jesus Christ told a parable about another poor money manager. He is more famously known as the Prodigal Son.

[1] Charles Dickens, A Christmas Carol, (London, Bradbury and Evans)

> *Jesus continued: "There was a man who had two sons. The younger one said to his father, 'Father, give me my share of the estate.' So he divided his property between them. Not long after that, the younger son got together all he had, set off for a distant country and there **squandered** his wealth in **wild** living. After he had **spent everything**, there was a severe famine in that whole country, and he began to be in **need**. So he went and hired himself out to a citizen of that country, who sent him to his fields to feed pigs. He longed to fill his stomach with the pods that the pigs were eating, but no one gave him anything. When he came to his senses, he said, 'How many of my father's hired men have food to spare, and here I am starving to death! I will set out and go back to my father and say to him: Father, I have sinned against heaven and against you. I am no longer worthy to be called your son; make me like one of your hired men.' So he got up and went to his father."*

Luke 15:11-20 – New International Version

The Prodigal's money management method can be easily analyzed by looking at four words.

- *Squandered* – *In New Testament times the word Luke used was an agricultural term associated with winnowing. Winnowing involved tossing wheat in the air with the goal of the chaff being blown away by a breeze. In effect the Prodigal was tossing his inheritance into thin air.*

- *Wild* – *The King James Version uses a word that I believe conveys the message a little more effectively than modern versions; riotous. It was also used to convey a sense of living without thinking, or living without being concerned.*

- *Spent* – *Once again, the original thought was much deeper than simply making too many purchases. The Prodigal spent all of his money but received no benefit from it. He had plenty, but used it for no purpose.*

- *Everything* – *This means exactly as it appears. It was all gone!*

- *Need* – *All of his "riotous" living had left the young man destitute.*

The Prodigal's money management had led him to the poor house. Actually, it led him past the poor house, for he found himself living and eating with pigs.

I find it interesting that these two characters took completely opposite paths but ended up in virtually the same circumstances. One, the spendthrift Prodigal, came to his senses mired in mud. The other, the penny-pinching Scrooge, came out of his nightmare, clutching and clinging to his bed post. One came to his point of need by spending every penny he had; the other by holding on to every cent as tightly as he could.

Churches should be careful not to resemble either one of these two behaviors. Some churches go overboard in developing cash disbursement controls and cling selfishly to their assets by making expenditures extremely difficult and cumbersome. Others place a premium on having reserve funds available for emergencies. While strong controls and emergency funds should be a part of cash management, a church should remember that God entrusts His church with funds for the purpose of growing the Kingdom, not amassing big savings accounts. Every church must be careful not to turn into a Scrooge, because when this happens they may find themselves cash rich but ministry poor.

On the other hand, churches should not resemble the Prodigal Son either. Spending without thinking may result in the exhaustion of the church's resources and the postponement, or in worst cases, the termination of a ministry.

Just like Ebenezer Scrooge and the Prodigal Son, churches operating on the extremes end up in virtually the same place, a dead or dying ministry. What is needed is something in the middle. A church should develop a rational plan to expend its resources, giving equal weight to accountability and ministry effectiveness. This is not only good stewardship; it is also good fraud protection.

A point that must not be forgotten is that just because the tithes and offerings have been safely brought into the "storehouse" does not mean the church is safe from financial harm. If fact many, if not most, of the largest frauds occur in the cash disbursement processes, not the cash receipts.

Same song, second verse...

Fraud prevention over cash disbursements follows the same cardinal principle used in managing cash receipts. Money, or access to it, should never be in the possession of one individual, regardless of the brevity of time. The only difference between these two areas of fraud prevention is the direction; outflow as compared with inflow.

Every church should perform a periodic fraud assessment of its cash disbursements with the objective of identifying and strengthening weak spots. Weak spots consist of any place along the church's cash "outflow" path (disbursements) where one individual can help himself to the church's money.

Have a plan in mind...

In order to be effective, a fraud prevention program must be intentional. Safe and secure churches do not happen by chance. Fraud-free churches plan and organize themselves to avoid financial bad behavior. This usually starts with a good plan. A strong fraud-resistant cash disbursement plan will have several characteristics.

First, any good plan will be put in writing. Putting a cash disbursement plan in writing will give the plan credibility. A written strategy will also serve as a baseline of expectations, helping the church to create the proper organizational tone. Putting the plan in writing also is a form of communication. In order for the plan to work effectively, everyone needs to know that it exists, what is in it, and understand that they are expected to implement it. A written plan will also enhance consistency in operations reducing the likelihood of mistakes and miscommunications.

The cash disbursement plan must also be comprehensive. Comprehensive means it should cover all of the steps from the initial approval of an order for goods or services to the filing of paid invoices. Of course, the church should strive for balance in this regard, because too much detail can serve to inhibit a church's ministry. This determination of balance can only be made at the local church level and is subject to the culture of the individual church involved.

With these two criteria in mind, a cash disbursement program will contain at least three major tasks:

- ❧ The establishment of a formal bill *approval* process.
- ❧ The establishment of secure bill paying processes.
- ❧ The provision of accountability.

The approval process...

In the Old Testament wicked King Ahab of Israel pressured Judah's King Jehoshaphat to join forces with him in battle. However, Jehoshaphat first wanted to check the Lord's will and asked if Israel had a prophet they could inquire of. Ahab's response: "There is one, but he never says anything good about me, only bad!"

Ahab's attitude is reminiscent of the attitudes some church staff and volunteers have toward their church's business manager. To these individuals, their church does not have an approval process. It has a "denial" process!

This is unfortunate, because a formal process of approving bills, *before the goods are ordered*, forms the foundation that the entire cash disbursement process rests upon. Ignoring or ridiculing the need for a formal approval process will almost automatically propel a church into a "Prodigal Son" lifestyle. No approval system is the first step in spending without thinking. But, a formal system will provide several helpful levels of protection. All churches should take steps to implement a formal approval system.

The first step is to assign responsibility for making purchasing decisions to individual staff members or volunteers within the church. Who and how many are questions that can only be answered at the local church level based on the church's culture and governance structure. Once again, balance should be a prime consideration. For example, if only one person can approve bills, efficiency may be lost and the church will have a difficult time carrying out its mission. On the other hand, if anyone and everyone can authorize the incurrence of expenses, control is lost.

Once decisions have been made as to who can authorize pur-chases, the church should then devise a plan to determine who it will do business with. Churches, especially as they grow in size, should administer its cash disbursements by using a "qualified vendor" list. What this means is that the church will not enter into any business transactions with a vendor until sufficient background information is obtained. For example, prior to placing orders with a company a church might want to know how long the vendor has been in business, who its principal ownership is, and who else the company does busi-ness with. Knowing the potential vendor's reputation in the commu-nity is important because if things go wrong, the church's reputation may be at risk. Once this information is obtained, the vendor is placed on an "approved vendor" list from which purchasing decisions will be made. Additionally, for expenditures of a more material nature, a church might consider utilizing a bidding process.

Once the participants in the process have been determined, the church should devise a plan that will document the transaction process. This is usually accomplished by using some form of purchase order system. If a manual system is to be employed, it is best to use pre-printed and sequentially numbered purchase orders. The forms should clearly reflect what was ordered, how much was ordered, the unit cost and who authorized the purchases. This process can also be accomplished electronically and most church management software systems include a purchasing module.

The final step may be the most important. After going to all of the trouble of assigning responsibility, screening vendors and preparing purchase orders, the process must be applied. Too often purchase orders are treated as routine and never amount to anything but a "paper chase." In order for them to work they must be used. This means comparing them to receiving records and billing invoices. It cannot be stated emphatically enough: If a church chooses not to use its purchase orders, the auditors are not the only ones who will notice. Fraudsters have a keen sense of when a victim's guard may be down.

Somebody has got to pay the bills...

In addition to the approval process, consistency must be a characteristic of bill paying too. To the best of its ability, a church should limit itself to one method of paying bills. Cash payments and credit card charges should be rare, rather than the main method of transacting business.[2] The reason for this exclusivity is that "normal" must be defined. Otherwise, how else will anyone ever know how to detect abnormal behavior? If the bill paying system is multi-faceted or changes daily, money can easily be misdirected to the wrong places.

A consistent bill paying process includes several key components:

[2]In recent years some churches, due to premiums offered by their bank, are engaging in cash management systems in which the majority of expenses are paid through credit card purchases. When properly managed, this can prove to be an effective cash disbursement system. This discussion does not refer to these types of situations.

- *Segregation of duties* – *At this point it is good to repeat the cardinal principle: Money should never be in the possession or control of a single individual. Bill paying tasks should be distributed among as many people as possible. The participants can consist of paid staff or volunteers.*

- *A strong, well documented check-writing process* – *The following steps, at a minimum, should be taken to insure that no bogus disbursements make it through the church system.*

  - *Keep the unused check stock locked in a secure location, such as a safe.*

  - *Use pre-printed and pre-numbered checks.*

- *Write checks in numerical sequence and account for the numbers at least monthly.*

  - *Prohibit the signing of blank checks.*

  - *Do not allow checks to be signed unless they are accompanied by the supporting documentation. (Purchase order and vendor invoice)*

  - *Consider requiring dual signature of checks above a certain dollar threshold.*[3]

  - *Perform a review of authorized check signers periodically.*

  - *Do not allow the checks to be mailed by the individual who prepared the checks or the individual responsible for general ledger and financial statement management.*

[3] This is one of the most overrated security steps. While the requirement for dual signatures enhances an already strong system, the reliance on this and nothing else is not much more effective than Linus' security blanket. Case in point; if this is the only security measure and the church hires a bookkeeper courageous enough to forge signatures no amount of signatures will be sufficient!

By implementing these steps a church will be well on its way to building a strong fraud protection wall against theft of cash in its cash disbursements processes. But don't be fooled. There is one more ingredient necessary. All of these measures will prove pointless if one more accountability step is left out.

Calling us to account...

The bank account reconciliation is the Grand Central Station of a church's accounting system. Every transaction flows through the bank reconciliation. Because of this, even though it is after the fact, the single most effective fraud prevention technique is accomplished through a thorough bank reconciliation process. Having the bank reconciliation performed by someone outside the normal day-to-day accounting processes provides a significant level of accountability. Knowing that at least once a month the bank activity is going to be looked at closely, will cause a thief to think twice about stealing from a church. Also, with the advent of online banking, the reconciliation process can be done almost at will eliminating the ability of a thief to time his behavior.

However, in order for a bank reconciliation to serve as a true deterrent, it must be done correctly. First, it needs to be understood that what we are not talking about is balancing the checkbook. While balancing is part of the process, it is not nearly the whole story, as a true reconciliation is not only concerned with the ending cash balance amount but also with the transactions entered involved in creating the cash amount. At a minimum, a bank reconciliation that provides accountability has the following steps:

- A comparison of dates and deposit amounts with count team reports.
- Investigation and documentation of transfers between bank accounts.
- Accounting for the sequence numbers of checks written.
- Examination of cancelled checks for suspicious signatures, endorsements or other alterations.
- Comparison of payees on cancelled checks with the approved vendor list
- Review of voided checks.

Segregation of duties is of utmost importance here. If the bookkeeper is also doing the reconciliation nothing much has been accomplished. Ideally, the person performing the reconciliation should be "outside the loop" as far as day-to-day transactions are concerned. This means that count team members, check signers, and the bookkeeper/accountant should not be the reconcilers. Also, keep in mind that another way bank reconciliations help prevent fraud is that they send a strong message. Requiring independent bank reconciliations is a clear statement that the church is serious about accountability. In most cases this statement alone will be sufficient to ward off the wolves.

Recent headlines...

Can I have your autograph?

ABC CHURCH WAS IMPRESSED WITH THE ABILITIES OF SUZI SMITH. AS HER CLERICAL AND BOOKKEEPING SKILLS BECAME MORE APPARENT, ADDITIONAL DUTIES WERE ASSIGNED TO HER. EVENTUALLY, SHE WAS GIVEN ALL

BOOKKEEPING DUTIES WITH THE EXCEPTION OF SIGNING CHECKS. THE CHURCH'S CONTROLS OVER CASH DISBURSE-MENTS CONSISTED SOLELY OF REQUIRING DUAL SIGNATURES FOR ALL CHECKS GREATER THAN $500. UNFORTUNATELY, THE CHURCH WAS UNAWARE OF ANOTHER OF SUZI'S SKILLS, HANDWRITING. ONLY AFTER SHE WAS STRICKEN WITH EMERGENCY SURGERY DID THE CHURCH DISCOVER THAT SHE HAD FORGED MORE THAN $150,000 IN CHECKS OVER A TEN YEAR PERIOD. BECAUSE SHE HAD TOTAL CONTROL OVER THE GENERAL LEDGER, FINANCIAL STATEMENTS AND BANK RECONCILIATION, SHE WAS ABLE TO COVER HER TRACKS; UNTIL HER UNFORTUNATE ILLNESS.

If only the church had taken the finance committee chairman up on his offer to perform a monthly bank reconciliation and disbursement review.

Too busy to pay attention…

BILL SMITH WAS THE BUSINESS ADMINISTRATOR OF HIS CHURCH. IT IS AN UNDERSTATEMENT TO SAY THAT BILL WAS A BUSY MAN. BECAUSE OF HIS HECTIC SCHEDULE, CHECK SIGNING BECAME ALMOST A FORMALITY. NOTICING THAT BILL SCARCELY LOOKED AT THE SUPPORTING DOCU-MENTATION ACCOMPANYING THE CHECKS PRESENTED FOR PAYMENT, HIS FINANCIAL SECRETARY BEGAN TO SIMPLY PRESENT HIM WITH THE CHECKS TO SIGN. HE APPRECIATED THIS BECAUSE IT SAVED HIM TIME AND HE WAS CERTAIN HE COULD TRUST HIS ASSISTANT. UNFORTUNATELY, THE ASSIS-TANT'S HUSBAND LOST HIS JOB AND THEY WERE UNABLE TO PAY THEIR CREDIT CARD BILL. SHE PROCEEDED TO OPEN A NEW ACCOUNT WITH THE SAME CREDIT CARD COMPANY

THE CHURCH USED AND ROLLED HER BALANCE INTO THE NEW ACCOUNT. SHE THEN PAID BOTH BILLS, HERS AND THE CHURCHES, WITH A CHURCH CHECK SIGNED BY BILL.

If only this church had written guidelines requiring all pay documentation to be accompanied with checks written for payment.

You need to do your research...

THE DIRECTOR OF MAINTENANCE OF BROOKVIEW COMMUNITY FELLOWSHIP WAS GIVEN COMPLETE RESPONSIBILITY TO SELECT VENDORS PROVIDING SERVICES TO THE CHURCH. HE ALSO WAS GIVEN PURCHASE APPROVAL FOR ALL EXPENDITURES IN HIS BUDGET AREA. OVER THE COURSE OF SEVERAL YEARS HE SET UP THREE FICTITIOUS COMPANIES AND PERIODICALLY SUBMITTED BOGUS INVOICES FOR HVAC MAINTENANCE, CUSTODIAL SERVICES AND BUILDING SUPPLIES. BEFORE HE WAS CAUGHT (THROUGH A TIP GIVEN BY A VENDOR) HE HAD MADE OFF WITH MORE THAN $100,000.

If only this church had a purchasing process that included screening of potential vendors in which pertinent information was obtained and evaluated such as Employer ID numbers, contact information and background references.

Five point fraud prevention test...

- *Has your church written a well defined and comprehensive purchase approval and bill paying program?*

- *Does your church require the use of pre-printed, numerically sequenced purchase orders for cash disbursements?*

- *Does your church prohibit check signers from participating in check preparation and/or recording processes?*

- *Are your church's bank reconciliations performed by an individual not involved in the day-to-day check writing and bookkeeping functions?*

- *Does your church have a vendor application process where potential providers of goods and services are screened before being utilized by the church?*

Chapter 10

Do You Know Who Your People Are?
(There are too such things as ghosts!)

'Call the workers and pay them their wages, beginning with the last ones hired and going on to the first.'

Matthew 20:8, New International Version

Principle - Churches who do not manage their personnel and payroll functions properly may be haunted by "ghost employees."

Although it has since become a major city with hundreds of thousands of residents, the town I grew up in was at one time part of rural America. Before the General Motors plant came to town, Arlington's primary industry was ginning cotton. Many of my boyhood friends and I spent a great deal of time exploring the surrounding countryside. Even though we were exactly halfway between Fort Worth and Dallas, at that time much of the surrounding areas remained in its natural state. It was a wilderness with the opportunity for adventure to most young boys with creeks, forests, and mysterious country roads.

Another opportunity for adventure of growing up in this rural setting was the presence of haunted houses. Any house or structure that was abandoned for at least a year or two was assumed to be haunted. And Arlington, like most rural towns going through "suburbanization," had an increasing number of old and abandoned structures, each one probably haunted and something to avoid. We weren't limited to haunted houses however, as I recall exploring, very carefully, a haunted chapel, a haunted school house, a haunted chicken coop and a haunted plantation.

What made these worrisome places so intriguing were the weird things that allegedly took place in them. We were convinced these places were inhabited by ghosts; spirits of the deceased who were former residents or owners of the haunted structures. The hauntings were always the result of some tragic event that had taken place in the haunted house's past. For example, the haunted chapel was a small, abandoned house of prayer located next to a small cemetery. In the early nineteenth century, the chapel and cemetery were part of a "home for un-wed mothers" as adoption houses used to be known. The cemetery consisted primarily of graves of infants who died during childbirth. Many of the grave markers said nothing more than Infant Number 51, etc. As the story was told, some nights a "woman" could be seen weeping and praying for one of the numbered infants lying nearby. I never knew anyone who ever saw this, but that didn't stop me from believing. In addition to the chapel, we would carefully explore an abandoned school house haunted by a jilted school master, a chicken coop haunted by a couple who lost their lives in a fire trying to free their chickens, and a plantation house, haunted by a slave brutally beaten by his master. The slave took his vengeance by reading at his former master's desk by the light of a kerosene lamp. I did see the lamp burning one night, but not the slave. But, that was enough to convince me that every bit of the story was true.

Much of this imagination was stoked by reading *The Adventures of Tom Sawyer*. In fact, the book was an essential reference tool for a proper understanding of the inner workings of haunted houses. In Tom Sawyer's opinion, haunted houses were the best places to hide buried treasure because very few people were brave enough to venture near them. There was no better evidence of this than Tom's pal, Huck Finn, who believed there had to be much better places to look for buried treasure. It took a great deal of convincing to get Huck to go to the haunted house. According to Huck Finn, haunted houses were filled with ghosts, who were a "dern site wors'n dead people. They slide around in a shroud and peep over your shoulder when you ain't lookin." [1]

But, Tom had answers for Huck's objections. Ghosts only "traveled around at night" and seeing as they were going during the day, there was nothing to worry about. And even if they went at night, nothing much ever happened there other than some "blue lights slipping by the windows." There were no "regular ghosts" ever seen around the house. Huck finally relented but only after letting Tom know that he reckoned "they were taking chances."

All of this conversation took place as they walked in the moonlight towards the haunted house. But, when they came upon the house, they stopped to see if they could see any blue lights. Then, they headed home and "struck far off to the right to give the haunted house a wide berth!"

It was stories like this that gave credence to many of the legends in my town. But, somewhere along the way I quit believing in ghosts. That is until I became involved in helping churches avoid fraud. At that point I quickly learned that quite a few churches are haunted. They are inhabited by "phantom employees."

[1] Mark Twain, The Adventures of Tom Sawyer, (New York, NY: Penguin Books)

You probably will never see a ghost employee...

"Phantom" or "ghost" employees are not like the ghosts Tom and Huck described. They generally do not wear shrouds or flash blue lights on window panes. In fact, ghost employees are seldom seen because most of them never darken the door of a church. But, in some mysterious and difficult to explain way, ghost employees are able to enter their time worked, receive a paycheck and convert the check to cash!
Yet, there is nothing supernatural about these phantoms. They are a figment of somebody's imagination. Ghost employees are fictitious employees whose paychecks are claimed by their creators. These ghosts usually come in two forms: a completely made-up employee, or a previous employee who has left the employment of the church, but with a little help, continues to receive a paycheck.

A haunted church is a church that does not take the time or make the effort to know who its employees are. If this practice goes on for a lengthy period of time, a church could end up with ghosts swarming its payroll system.

The church's largest target...

Personnel costs are the single largest category of expense of most churches. Salaries, wages, taxes, health insurance, and other benefits will account for anywhere from forty to fifty-five percent of a church's annual budget. This is understandable because, in business terms at least, churches are engaged in the "service" industry.

There are several good reasons why a church should be serious about personnel management. First, it makes good sense from a management perspective because solid personnel organization provides quality leadership and consistent treatment of a church's most valuable asset, its people. Being intentional in making good personnel decisions provides direction to the church and reduces the likelihood of "malcontents" who have a tendency to undercut the ministry.

A second reason why strong personnel policies are important is that following a "best practices" approach of personnel administration helps keep the church out of trouble with the IRS, the Department of Labor and other governmental agencies. Failure to abide by the rules, even if due to mistake, can severely impair a church, and in extreme cases terminate a ministry.

A third reason for practicing good personnel management is that by doing so some huge fraud weak spots can be closed down. Because personnel costs are the largest expense of a church, this area is a favorite target of thieves for two very good reasons. First is the obvious reason; there is simply more money to steal here. Second, it is easier to cover up tracks within the big numbers as relatively small anomalies in the system may go unnoticed.

Steps in avoiding payroll fraud...

Assign responsibility. Nothing of any value happens by accident. In order to avoid being hit by payroll fraud a church must take *intentional* steps to set up a system resistant to it. The first thing that must be done is to clearly assign responsibility for various tasks throughout the church.

A personnel committee or team should be given responsibility to set policy and provide administrative oversight of the church's human resources activities. One of this group's most important tasks is the setting of salaries, documenting their decisions and performing market comparison surveys for executive employee compensation in order to stay in compliance with tax laws. Additionally, the personnel team should be responsible for payroll administration and benefits management.

Employees must also have a clear understanding of what their responsibilities are. Two steps are involved in doing this. First, on an overall basis, the general expectations and practices of the church should be communicated to employees, preferably though a comprehensive personnel manual. Second, on an individual basis, churches should create and use written job descriptions so that each employee will have a clear understanding of what their duties and responsibilities are.

By having a well documented method of assigning responsibility, a church takes a strong step towards fraud protection because taking the time to assess and assign helps the church in the next step of payroll fraud prevention.

Implement measures to help know who your people are. Phantom employees will not take up residence in a church that makes a strong effort to know who its employees are and adequately documents this knowledge. This "getting to know you" process needs to start well before the individual becomes an employee of the church. Waiting until later may prove to be extremely costly.

    ❦ First, a church should perform a background check on all potential new-hires. This has become quite common in recent years due to the well documented and unfortunate child abuse situations that have plagued the church world. However, in addition to criminal background checks many churches are performing credit checks on potential employees, particularly employees handling cash or performing other financial tasks. A common theme of many fraud cases is that the crimes are not committed by "criminals" in the normal sense. They are committed by normal people in some type of financial trouble, who cannot resist taking from their employer to save themselves. Churches should keep in mind that if they hire an individual with bad credit the church will often inherit the problems. It is a good thing to know this up front so that the problem can be addressed, or another applicant chosen to fill the position.

ὠ Second, the church compensation committee should be involved, to some degree, in all hiring decisions. In many cases where churches have been hit by ghost employees, the personnel team, and senior management had limited knowledge of how the hiring process was taking place. This lack of knowledge makes it very easy for supervisory employees to add fictitious employees to the payroll list. Of course for large churches, it would be impossible for a personnel or compensation committee to be involved in every hiring decision. In those cases a regular, formal, and detailed review could be performed to broadcast the message that the church is watching.

To document its knowledge of its workforce the church should maintain personnel files for each employee. No paycheck should be issued to new employees until a comprehensive employee file has been created.

Each file should have the following characteristics:

> - *Up-to-date* – *Someone must have responsibility for making sure that files are maintained on a current basis. Incredibly, it sometimes may be better to have no files, rather than having ones with outdated information.*
>
> - *Complete* – *Sufficient effort should be taken to insure that the church obtains ALL of the necessary documents to both establish identity of the employee and be in compliance with payroll regulations. Items included should be applications, W-4 forms, immigration forms, and payroll deduction authorizations.*
>
> - *Secured* - *The payroll files MUST be locked in a secured location. By being lax in this area a church not only exposes itself to charges of breach in confidentiality, it also makes it easier to create bogus employees.*

🥀 Finally, churches must know its employees until the bitter end. That will involve requiring written termination letters to be obtained from all departing employees. Also, when possible, exit conferences should be held with the departing employees.

Make "payday" a "safe day." To make sure that the church's money goes to the right people the following steps should be taken.

🥀 Although ministerial positions in a church are normally paid on a salary basis, most churches have a significant number of other employees who are paid on an hourly basis. This is especially true for churches that operate daycare, afterschool programs and private schools. For hourly employees, especially if the church operates one of these satellite ministries, time worked should be accumulated by a sophisticated system such as computer based "swipe" cards, or a time clock and punch cards. Also, the timekeeping functions and paycheck preparation duties should be separated. Not only does this make things more difficult to create a ghost employee, it also assists the church in maintaining adequate wage and hour requirements documentation.

🕮 Too often the "tyranny of the urgent" is the philosophy that governs church management. When this is the case, decisions are made simply by how quickly the job can be done. Unfortunately, this can occur with payroll preparation and when it does, payrolls can be prepared and checks distributed with no supervisory review taking place. Thieves can sniff these situations out and if they determine that "no one is looking," they can hatch a myriad of schemes to dip into the church's pocketbook. To avoid this, payroll procedures should include a review of the payroll journal and paycheck information by the church business administrator, or other supervisory individual, prior to paycheck distribution or release of funds for direct deposit.

A few effective review steps are:

> • *Periodically compare an employee list with the payroll journal.*
>
> • *Quarterly reconcile the total payroll expense on the church's financial statements with the amount reported on the quarterly 941 report.*
>
> • *Annually reconcile the total salary on the church's financial statements with the W-2 forms issued to employees.*
>
> • *Periodically sort payroll data to search for duplicate addresses, social security numbers and last names.*
>
> • *Seriously investigate unclaimed paychecks or W-2 forms.*

One other step a church might consider is to conduct a surprise paycheck distribution. In these situations, in order to claim their paycheck, an employee must present proof of identification to a designated paymaster. At the end of the day, any unclaimed paychecks would be turned over to the church business administrator or personnel committee. Unfortunately, one of the negative by-products of technology is that many employers no longer issue paychecks, instead directly depositing pay into the bank accounts of their employees. This new efficiency had rendered the surprise paycheck distribution ineffective. However, this step could be modified by requiring all employees to present identification to obtain a W-4 at the beginning of the year, or to obtain their W-2 at the end of the year.

I ain't afraid of no ghosts...

The day after their moonwalk stroll by the haunted house, Tom and Huck headed back to look for the buried treasure. But along the way, Huck asked Tom what day it was. When Tom realized it was Friday he knew immediately they could not go into the house. Fridays were not good luck days. Saying that "a body can't be too careful" the boys postponed their excursion until Saturday. They were still afraid. But Saturday came and they returned to the house. As they quietly crept into the house and slowly took things in, "familiarity modified their fears." Likewise, churches do not need to fear employee ghosts if they will simply get familiar with their employees and their payroll system.

Recent headlines...

Garbage in, garbage out...

A WOMAN WHO ADMITTED STEALING MORE THAN $500,000 FROM ST. MATTHEW'S CHURCH WAS SENTENCED TO SEVEN YEARS IN PRISON YESTERDAY. AS PART OF THE SENTENCE SHE MUST PAY THE MONEY BACK. THE WOMAN WAS EMPLOYED BY THE CHURCH AS ITS BOOKKEEPER AND HAD SOLE RESPONSIBILITY FOR PAYROLL PREPARATION. SHE PLEAD GUILTY TO *SUBMITTING INFLATED SALARY FIGURES FOR HERSELF* TO THE CHURCH'S PAYROLL PROCESSING COMPANY. SHE CONCEALED THE THEFT BY ALTERING TAX RECORDS AND CHURCH INTERNAL REPORTS.

If only this church had required all payroll information to be reviewed by the church administrator or a member of the payroll committee prior to submission of payroll data to its payroll service provider

Her memory failed her...

THE FINANCIAL ADMINISTRATOR OF MAYFIELD COMMUNITY OF FAITH HAS BEEN ARRESTED AND CHARGED WITH THEFT AFTER BEING ACCUSED OF EMBEZZLING MORE THAN $100,000. THE ADMINISTRATOR'S THEFTS CAME TO LIGHT WHEN AUDITORS DISCOVERED AN UNAUTHORIZED PAYROLL CHECK WRITTEN BY THE ADMINISTRATOR TO HERSELF IN THE AMOUNT OF $2,000. HER INITIAL EXPLANATION WAS THAT SHE HAD SIMPLY PAID HERSELF AN ADVANCE AND FORGOTTEN TO PAY THE MONEY BACK. FURTHER INVESTIGATION BY THE AUDITORS HELPED THE ADMINISTRATOR REMEMBER ANOTHER $98,000 IN FRAUDULENT PAYROLL CHECKS.

If only this church had assigned payroll processing duties to several different people. Also, a quarterly reconciliation of the federal quarterly reports, payroll journal and general ledger would probably have turned up the scam much sooner.

The haunted church...

FOR THE FIRST TIME, HARMONY CHURCH HELD A CHRISTMAS LUNCHEON FOR ALL OF ITS EMPLOYEES INCLUDING THE PART-TIME STAFF OF THE CHURCH'S PRE-SCHOOL PROGRAM. PASTOR JONES WAS PUZZLED BY THE FACT THAT ONLY TWELVE OF THE TWENTY FIVE PRE-SCHOOL PROGRAM EMPLOYEES ATTENDED THE PARTY. HE ASKED THE DIRECTOR

WHY MORE THAN HALF OF THE EMPLOYEES SKIPPED THE PARTY AND WAS TOLD A "BUG" WAS GOING THROUGH THE SCHOOL. CONCERNED, THE PASTOR ASKED FOR PHONE NUMBERS OF THE ABSENTEES SO HE COULD CALL ON HIS ILL EMPLOYEES.... BY THE TIME HE HAD GOTTEN TO THE BOTTOM OF HIS LIST HE HAD LEARNED THAT THE THIRTEEN ILL EMPLOYEES DID NOT EXIST, BUT WERE GHOST EMPLOYEES CREATED BY THE DIRECTOR WHO POCKETED NEARLY $150,000 OVER HER TENURE AS DIRECTOR.

If this church had only once a year conducted a surprise paycheck distribution requiring paychecks to be picked up in the pastor or business administrator's office upon presentation of a valid identification.

Five point fraud prevention test...

- *Has your church formally assigned payroll and personnel responsibilities to a compensation or personnel committee?*

- *Does your church maintain up-to-date, complete, and secure personnel files? Is the process inventoried at least annually?*

- *If hourly employees are a significant portion of your church's workforce, does the church use a sophisticated timekeeping system like swipe cards or punch cards and separate the timekeeping and payroll processing functions?*

- *Is payroll data reviewed by a responsible individual outside of the payroll department prior to submission to the church's payroll service provider?*

- *Do your church's payroll processes include reconciliation of the payroll journal, quarterly tax reports and general ledger on at least a quarterly basis?*

Chapter 11

ℐs Anyone Watching Over Your Stuff?

Be on guard! Be alert! You do not know when that time will come. It's like a man going away: He leaves his house and puts his servants in charge, each with his assigned task, and tells the one at the door to keep watch.

Mark 13:33-34, New International Version

Principle - "Unwatched" furniture, fixtures and equipment might just grow legs and wander off.

In the film, *National Treasure*, Benjamin Franklin Gates, travels to the Arctic searching for a legendary treasure from the American Revolutionary period. He discovers another riddle, stuffed in a barrel full of gun powder, in an ice encased ship named the Charlotte:

> "The legend writ,
> The stain affected
> The key in silence undetected.
> Fifty-five in iron pen,
> Mr. Matlack can't offend..."[1]

Displaying an incredible aptitude in deductive reasoning, Ben Gates solves the riddle. The iron did not refer to the pen or the ink, but the strength of the words being written. "Matlack" refers to one Timothy Matlack who served as the official scribe of the Continental Congress.

[1] National Treasure, Walt Disney Pictures, 2004

Matlack created a document signed by fifty-five men. The Declaration of Independence! The "legend writ" must refer to a treasure map hidden on the back of the Declaration of Independence so that Mr. Matlack would not accidentally deface it when copying our nation's first official document. Only in the movies!

The movie's villain, Ian suggests they go to Washington and "borrow" the Declaration of Independence. Ben, although having a reputation of being a conspiracy kook, is a patriot. Opposed to the idea on principal, he refuses. Deciding that he no longer has use for Ben, Ian leaves Ben and his sidekick, Riley Poole, trapped in the ship and heads to Washington to steal the Declaration of Independence.

Ben miraculously survives the explosion of the ship's two hundred year old gun powder supply, (Remember this is a movie!) and is determined to stop the theft. He returns to Washington only to be discounted as a nut by the FBI. Not giving up, Ben goes to the National Archives to warn them that the Declaration of Independence was at considerable risk. But, when he tells the director a treasure map is on the back of the document, once again he is classified as a kook.

Before leaving, Ben and Riley spend a few minutes with the other tourists looking at our nation's founding document. Ben is overcome with patriotism and decides that he must protect the Declaration of Independence; by stealing it!

Initially, Riley would hear nothing of it, pointing out that in addition to the fact that such a thing *should* not be done, it also *could* not be done. To prove his point he takes Ben to the Library of Congress and shows him the blueprints, phone lines and the water and sewer system of the National Archives building. He also describes the great pains the government goes to in order to protect the Declaration.

When the document is on display it is constantly surrounded by guards, video monitors and "little families from Iowa." The Declaration of Independence sits in a case made up of one inch thick bullet-proof glass. The case contains an army of sensors and heat monitors that will go off if someone "with a high fever gets too close to the glass!"

Protective measures are enhanced when the Declaration is not on display. It is lowered into a four foot thick concrete and steel plated vault. To keep intruders away the vault is locked with an electronic combination lock and armed with a biometric access denial system. Our government is serious about protecting its "stuff."

However, Ben Gates was not that impressed and calls to mind Thomas Edison and his more than two thousand failed attempts to create a light bulb. Edison was never discouraged with these "failures" because he knew he only had to find one way to make his invention work. And he knew he would find it.

Ben Gates was not impressed with the "thousands" of reasons Riley gave as to why stealing the document could not be done. He knew he had to only find one way to do it. And he thought he had found the one weak spot in the government's protection; the preservation room. When maintenance was required on the document or its protection system, the case containing the Declaration of Independence is taken from the vault to the preservation room where there is far less security.

Ben decides to strike during an upcoming gala when the guards would be even further distracted. Ben and Riley go through an elaborate process to gain entry, including compromising the security cameras, stealing passwords and fingerprints, engaging in identity theft, and setting off sensors so the case would make its way to the preservation room. After ciphering the director's password, Ben is in. And sure enough, the Declaration is in the preservation room. ALONE!

Back to reality...

Ok, this is only a movie. I think we can rest assured that the Declaration of Independence is never alone. Even in the preservation room. The reality is this: the government may be pretty loose with its money. (Have you looked at the budget deficits lately?) But it is serious about keeping up with its "stuff."

Lessons learned...

There are three simple lessons that churches can learn from this.

- First, fraud is not just about money. Thieves want more than cash. They want your stuff, too.

- Second, a church's stuff, just like its cash, should never be left unprotected, even for the shortest times.

- And third, churches must be vigilant. In spite of elaborate protective steps that may be taken, they must remember the Edison rule. Crooks only need to find *one* way to get in. And they are constantly practicing and refining that craft.

Churches would do well to imitate the government, at least in this movie. Of course, I am not advocating bullet-proof glass and biotech access systems. But, even the smallest protective steps would put most churches ahead of the curve in this much neglected aspect of fraud prevention and protection.

What exactly do you mean by "stuff"?

Before we define "stuff" we need to first recall our discussion in Chapter Two about the three types of occupational fraud. One of the categories of fraud is termed *misappropriation of assets*. In the church environment most people think only of cash when they hear the term. But, misappropriation can happen with *non-cash* assets too. In fact, the Association of Certified Fraud Examiners' statistics reflect that this type of behavior is fairly frequent (16% of reported cases in their 2008 annual report) and relatively costly (median loss of $100,000). Misappropriation of non-cash assets can also take on several different forms as well. For instance, misappropriation of cash normally consists of one thing; theft. In addition to being stolen, non-cash assets can suffer misappropriation in the following manners:

- The most common type is general abuse and mistreatment. Most "company owned" assets devalue quickly because people do not take care of someone else's property like they do their own.

- Vandalism is a form of abuse that makes little sense to most of us because the perpetrators do not benefit financially. Instead, they gain some type of satisfaction from causing harm or seeing something destroyed. Whatever the reason, this form of asset misuse is extremely costly.

- Misappropriation of church non-cash assets can also involve how the property is used. Three ways this can occur that churches should try to avoid are:

    - Using the assets in a way contrary to the exempt purpose of mission of the church.

    - Using the assets for personal purposes.

¤ Using the assets in a criminal activity.

Churches have been taken advantage of and severely wounded by people using all of these methods of property abuse.

Church "stuff" varies from congregation to congregation because the types of assets churches purchase is a function of their individual ministry approach. For example, the fixed assets of a historic, traditional congregation will be completely different from a start-up, seeker congregation meeting in a school auditorium. As a result, fraud protection measures, risk management and asset stewardship programs must be custom-fitted to each particular church. The following list is a good reflection of the variety of non-cash assets found in churches across the world and a few things that could go wrong in their stewardship:

- **Buildings** - *Without question, buildings are the single largest asset purchase of most churches. Because they are a little too heavy to carry, misappropriation usually takes the form of improper use or vandalism. However, temporary structures have been known to disappear in the middle of the night.*

- **Furniture and fixtures** – *Because these assets are usually attached to the church building misappropriation of these assets is usually confined to vandalism.*

- **Computers, sound and media equipment** – *These types of assets are the most frequent target of fraudsters and can be misused in all three ways.*
  - ¤ *They suffer misuse and are frequently the targets of vandalism.*
  - ¤ *They are a favorite of thieves because they are movable and have a readily available market.*
  - ¤ *Because of their mobility, they can easily be used for non-church activities.*

- **Transportation equipment** – *Similar to the previous group, cars, trucks, and trailers are abused, stolen, and used improperly.*

- **Inventory of goods held for sale** – *Many churches operate bookstores, coffee shops, and thrift stores requiring them to maintain an inventory of goods held for sale. Not giving attention to the processes used in inventory management can result in theft and improper use of the items.*

- **Intellectual property** – *When discussing "stuff" most church's never think of creative assets such as sheet music, cds, dvds, and computer programs. If these assets are not protected in a fraud prevention plan, they can be stolen or even worse, duplicated.*

Keep in mind that this is just a sample of things churches own that thieves covet. Without doubt there are many more. The rule of thumb should be: if it is worth at least one hundred dollars and is not anchored to the building, it is fair game in the eyes of crooks. There is one other ingredient that makes these types of church assets attractive; they are seldom watched over closely by their owners!

How to stand guard over the church's property...

Assign responsibility - Just as with payroll, in order to avoid problems, someone has to be in charge. A facilities committee or team must be appointed and formally given the responsibility of stewardship over the church's fixed assets. Not placing authority and responsibility with a facilities oversight committee will almost certainly lead to inconsistent management and prove costly to the church. There are many tasks that could be given this group and the larger the church, the larger the task list. However, these three tasks should be formally assigned for all churches, regardless of size:

- ❧ The facilities committee should approve all significant acquisitions and disposals of fixed assets.

- ❧ The facilities committee should be responsible for facilities management. This involves developing, implementing and overseeing policies and procedures designed to manage asset usage, condition, security and location.

🕊 The facilities committee should be given the task of risk management, making sure that sufficient and appropriate insurance coverage is obtained and remains in force.

Adopt a formal equipment use policy. Probably the first step the facilities committee should take is to write and implement the church's facilities policies. A significant part of this package should be a facilities use policy. In order to protect its "stuff," each church must adopt policies dictating who can use church property and what it can be used for. Additionally, the policy must insure that all potential uses are in conformity with the church's exempt purpose. And, just like a personnel policy, this policy must be clearly communicated to the church staff and members. Little protection will exist if few people know such a policy exists. The policy should be accompanied by an adequate monitoring system allowing the church to be confident that it is living by its rules. This should include a process that clearly documents the checking out or reserving of assets.

Implement an equipment inventory program. Most churches do not have a clear idea of how many "things" they own. They would also be even more surprised to know how much they spend each year on equipment. But, because churches tend to be extremely budget driven, many asset purchases are simply "line-item" expenditures and a cost of doing business. Once the expenditure is made, and the church remains safely within budget, no further thought is given to the stewardship of the items purchased. It is probably safe to say that the most unused module of church management software systems is the fixed asset module.

To assist the church in keeping up with its equipment, a church should maintain detailed asset lists. The reason to do this can be summed up in one simple question. If the church does not know what it owns, how will it ever know if anything is missing? The answer is also simple: It won't! Maintaining a comprehensive and up-to-date list will go a long way in helping a church answer this question and more importantly possibly stop potential losses. The knowledge that a church keeps up with things can be a strong deterrent to a thief.

Combined with the listing should be an annual inventory of the property. Periodically, an inventory should be taken and the results compared with the church's asset lists. Some churches, particularly larger ones with numerous assets, rely on high-tech methods of developing an asset inventory, such as a tag and scanning process in which the assets are categorized by code. Another common method, and one that is helpful for insurance purposes, is a video walk through of the church premises. Taking inventory seems to have a weakness in that it is an "after the fact" action. On the surface it appears that it is a reporting device that only tells us what went missing, not how to stop it.

While partially true, believing that an annual inventory's only purpose is reporting what is missing ignores a major point. There is one thing a thief hates more than anything else, and that is getting caught! The fact that a church takes the time to keep a list and occasionally checks it against its property increases the odds that wrongdoing will be discovered. Eventually, the trail might lead to the crook. To avoid this, thieves will simply move down the street to another victim; believe me there are plenty of other candidates!

Develop a comprehensive security plan. No one wants to turn their church campus into Fortress God. The whole point of The Church is to reach out to the world with a healing and welcoming message of Good News. But times have changed and churches increasingly have to do things that a generation earlier would have been unthinkable. This includes establishing procedures to provide security to the church's property, employees, members and visitors. Some of these measures include prohibiting or restricting access to unused areas of the campus on weekdays, password access to other areas, and implementation of security cameras. These steps can be taken in a discreet manner while at the same time providing adequate security.

Recent headlines...

Do not take along any gold, silver or copper... (Matthew 10:9)

POLICE ARE LOOKING FOR A THIEF WHO WAS CAUGHT ON SURVEILLANCE VIDEO STEALING COPPER FROM THE AIR CONDITIONING UNITS AT ELM STREET COMMUNITY FELLOWSHIP. THE TAPE REVEALED A MAN BEHIND THE CHURCH BREAKING INTO SEVERAL AIR CONDITIONING UNITS. THE HEIST GARNERED THE THIEF APPROXIMATELY $250. HOWEVER, CHURCH OFFICIALS ESTIMATE REPAIR COSTS WILL EXCEED $5,000.

If only this church had implemented a comprehensive security program which included a provision restricting access to selected areas of the church campus, including the air conditioning units.

Prayer warrior...

POLICE ARE SEEKING A MAN WHO WAS GRANTED ENTRANCE TO BLUE WATER BAPTIST CHURCH TUESDAY AFTERNOON BY A CUSTODIAN AFTER SAYING HE NEEDED TO GO TO THE CHURCH SANCTUARY TO PRAY. WHILE MAKING HIS ROUNDS A FEW MINUTES LATER, THE CUSTODIAN NOTICED THE MAN WAS NOT IN THE SANCTUARY. THE CUSTODIAN CALLED AUTHORITIES WHO WERE UNABLE TO LOCATE

THE INTRUDER. A SUBSEQUENT SEARCH OF CHURCH PREMISES REVEALED THAT THREE COMPUTERS AND A VIDEO CAMERA WERE MISSING FROM THE CHURCH'S MEDIA ROOM.

If only this church followed a practice of prohibiting access to unused areas of the church campus, particularly on days when no church activities are taking place.

The copy cat...

A LOCAL MAN HAS BEEN TAKEN INTO CUSTODY AFTER BEING FOUND IN POSSESSION OF HUNDREDS OF COUNTERFEIT CDS, DVDS AND COMPUTER GAMES. THE MAN WAS ILLEGALLY COPYING AND SELLING THE PIRATED PRODUCTS ON HIS WEBPAGE. THE COUNTERFEIT PRODUCTS WERE PRODUCED ON DUPLICATING EQUIPMENT "BORROWED" FROM THE MAN'S EMPLOYER, CRESTVIEW COMMUNITY CHURCH.

If only this church had implemented an equipment use policy which included the following points:

- *A clear communication that church equipment could be used ONLY for church purposes.*
- *An equipment security program that stored assets in locked and monitored areas.*
- *A check-out system documenting asset use and their whereabouts.*

Five point fraud prevention test...

- *Has your church appointed a facilities committee responsible for property use and stewardship; risk management and security?*

- *Does your church maintain a detailed listing of its physical properties?*

- *Does your church annually take a physical inventory of its property and equipment to assess location and condition of the various items it owns?*

- *On days when the church is not conducting activities is access to the unused areas of the church campus restricted?*

- *Has your church adopted an equipment use policy and implemented a documented check-in/check-out process?*

Weeds in the Garden

Chapter 12

Have You Taken Any of This to Heart?

Apply your heart to instruction and your ears to words of knowledge.

Proverbs 23:12, New International Version

Principle – It is not enough to simply be aware of the threat of fraud or go through the motions of fraud prevention. Churches that don't commit themselves to a strong fraud prevention and detection program will likely end up as victims.

Maggie Carpenter had a problem with commitment. The opening scene in "Runaway Bride" makes this crystal clear. The scene opens with Maggie, played by Julia Roberts, riding a horse at full gallop. But what gives the visual so much impact is that she is wearing a brilliantly white wedding dress! It is obvious that she is not in a hurry to get to her wedding; she is fleeing for all she is worth. Soon, the movie reveals that this tendency to run is nothing new. According to one man, she had done it seven or eight times before.

Ike Graham, a New York newspaper columnist in search of a story, overhears the comment and realizes he has found his topic. He proceeds to write a very unflattering account of Maggie's lack of commitment and while he is at it, includes quite a few remarks offensive to most women.

It is never a good idea for a writer to offend half of his potential audience. Because of this and the inclusion of some "factual errors," the reporter is fired.

What was his error? Maggie had not run out on her groom seven or eight times. She had only done it three times… The first time she ran, she jumped on the back of a motorcycle and was whisked away. During her second "escape," Maggie was doing fine through the processional but abruptly decided to skip the ceremony and move immediately to the recessional. She dashed out of the church with the ring bearer clinging for dear life to the train of her second wedding gown. The third attempt ended in the horseback escape. At this point in the film, Maggie is in the midst of planning a wedding for the fourth time. The entire town and now, because of Ike's article, much of the nation, was on pins and needles wondering; "Will she, or won't she?"

In an attempt to resurrect his career, Ike Graham heads to Maggie's hometown to write a feature story. He wants a ringside seat, to see if the Runaway Bride would strike once again. Sure enough, she balks once more, this time because she has fallen in love with the reporter. Eventually she and Ike are married, but not until their second attempt. Their first wedding attempt closed with Maggie riding off into the sunset in a FedEx truck. Maggie Carpenter had a problem with commitment.

Another movie character, Rudy Ruettiger, was all about commitment. Rudy had a dream; he wanted more than anything else to play football for the Fighting Irish of Notre Dame. He dreamed of one day running through the tunnel and onto the turf at Notre Dame Stadium.

However, Rudy seemingly had everything stacked against him, starting with his size. Five foot seven and one hundred sixty-five pound guys can play high school football, but anyone that size trying to play major college football might get killed! Also, his inadequacies were not limited to physical qualities. Rudy had poor academic skills as well, which were later diagnosed as dyslexia. His grades were so poor that even if he had been big enough he would not be accepted by Notre Dame.

For most people, these two deficiencies alone would be enough to end any dreams like Rudy's. But, size and academics were not the only hurdles. Rudy was surrounded by dismissive coaches and family members who constantly told him to give up his dream. Poverty was an issue as well: being the third of fourteen children it was obvious that no "college fund" had been set aside by his parents. Nevertheless, Rudy held on to his dream.

More importantly, Rudy committed himself to seeing the dream become reality. He took on and overcame each and every hurdle that had been placed in his way. Rudy saved his money. He went to a junior college and brought his grades up. He worked as a grounds keeper to pay his way and nurture his dream. Eventually, the first phase of his goal was reached; he was accepted into Notre Dame.

In spite of his size, Rudy tried out for and made the Fighting Irish practice squad. For two seasons he helped the "real players" prepare for their upcoming opponents by practicing with the varsity. In the process, he took countless vicious hits and suffered numerous cuts and bruises. Through it all, he clung to his dream and eventually, he was allowed to suit up for the last game of his senior year. He even got to play a little too!

Rudy knew what he wanted and learned what it was going to take to get there. Most importantly, he committed himself to a plan to get there. And he succeeded.

Make a commitment to be fraud-free...

Every church needs to make a decision when it comes to their commitment to fraud protection. Are they going to be a Maggie, or are they going to be a Rudy? Will they step up to the plate and face down the challenge, or will they run from it?

Maggie probably knew more than most women about weddings. She had plenty of experience in selecting dresses, colors, flowers and wedding cakes. Without a doubt she knew how a wedding should work; processionals, music, vows, rings and recessionals. But when crunch time came, she would be overcome with fear, and run.

Similarly, just knowing that fraud can and does exist in churches is not enough. Neither is having a working understanding of the many ways and methods fraud is perpetrated. Many churches know every bit of this. But too many churches, like Maggie, run away when crunch time comes. Crunch time in this sense usually means opposition from church leaders and members who continue to believe the myth that "it can never happen here."

The key ingredient to fraud protection is commitment, because fraud prevention does not happen by accident; it takes effort. Every church needs to remember that the absence of fraud can usually be attributed to one of two things, luck or a strong commitment to fraud prevention. I would not recommend the luck method for one simple reason. Luck, if such a thing really exists, tends to run out. One day, in spite of the integrity of the church's staff and volunteers, something will probably go wrong. Not taking action is not a good plan.

A strong commitment on the other hand, like Rudy, enhances a church's chances of remaining free from the devastating effects of a fraud attack. This commitment is best exhibited by the creation of a formal fraud risk assessment and prevention program that requires the church to do the following six things.

Appoint – Fraud prevention is a team sport; no one should try to do this by themselves. Before putting one word or idea on paper, a church should first choose up sides. On one side, even though invisible, will be those wanting to take advantage of the church. To combat this foe, the church should appoint an anti-fraud team. This team's responsibility is to give direction to the church's fraud risk assessment process and provide oversight to the management of the church's fraud prevention measures. Preferably, a member of the church's senior staff would also be appointed as a liaison between church members, staff and committee members.

Assess – Before implementing policies, a church must first have a thorough understanding of its current condition. Determining where the church stands should be the first thing the fraud risk team accomplishes. The easiest way to do this is to reserve a Saturday morning and hold a brainstorming session. In the church environment the best way to start is by addressing four different concerns:

❧ How is the church's *"tone at the top"*? Is senior leadership fully committed with this? Does the church have policies in place that address compensation, related party transactions, expense reimbursements and credit card use for example? This is the beginning point, because if the answer to these questions is "no," procedures protecting revenues, expenses and payroll will be of little use.

🌿 Does the church have a good *understanding of all of its revenue streams?* Time should be spent to review all sources of revenue and the controls placed on them. Flow charting and organizational charting is extremely helpful in this process.

🌿 The same procedure should be performed on the "outflow" pipeline. The anti-fraud team needs to gain an *understanding of all of the ways the church spends its money.* This should be a comprehensive review and include cash payments, checks, credit cards, online payments, and electronic transfers. Flow charting and organizational charting is also of great benefit here as well.

🌿 *Who does the church employ* and how are they being paid? As pointed out in previous chapters, personnel costs are a favorite target of thieves. The anti-fraud team should review all of the procedures surrounding payroll including the church's practice of paying independent contractors.

It should be very obvious that this initial assessment will probably not be accomplished in one sitting. It will take several sessions to fully complete this task. But, the assessment lays the foundation for what is to follow and without it, success will probably be an illusion.

Create and implement – Once exposure to fraud has been assessed, attention can then be directed towards fraud prevention. The first step in fraud prevention is the creation and implementation of a well documented plan which lays out the various processes to be followed that will enhance fraud protection. The chapters in this book have been arranged in a way that can serve as the foundation for such a plan. Each of the chapters is representative of one area of church management crucial to the prevention of fraud. While the plan should be as comprehensive as possible, care should be taken to use concise language in order to eliminate the likelihood of misunderstanding

Communicate – Having a documented plan of fraud prevention is one thing, but using it is something altogether different. Too often, policy and procedure documents are created by organizations only to be set on a shelf and forgotten about. In order to be effective, a fraud prevention plan must be used. And the first step in utilization is communication. Church staff, officers, volunteers and members must know that the church has a fraud prevention plan in place. Also, it must be clearly communicated to staff that they are responsible for managing fraud in their assigned areas.

Monitor – Once the plan is created, implemented and communicated, it must be managed. As a result, the church anti-fraud team's role will change from design and implementation to monitoring. Some of the steps involved in this arena are:

🌿 Developing a reporting and review process. This can be a combination of internally generated reports, internal audit procedures and independent audits by Certified Public Accountants.

🌿 Establishing appropriate and safe channels through which sensitive information can be reported. An anonymous tip hotline is one example.

🌿 Developing a standard process for dealing with fraud incidents which includes:

¤ A thorough investigation of each fraud incident.

¤ Gaining a full understanding of how the breach occurred.

¤ Taking appropriate and consistent actions against perpetrators.

¤ Implementation of new measures to close down any weaknesses discovered.

¤ Full but appropriate communication to the church and staff of the incident.

Remain vigilant – All things in life change, including fraud techniques. While you are reading this book, you can be sure that thieves and crooks are working hard dreaming up new ways to take your church's money and property. No church can afford to sit back and relax. Churches must be constantly on the alert staying abreast of not only what goes on inside their own walls but what is going on in the culture as well.

The brainstorming exercise mentioned a few paragraphs earlier is not something to be done once. To be effective, a church's fraud prevention program should include an annual assessment of the church's vulnerability to fraud. The annual sessions normally will not be as lengthy and as in-depth as the original, but are necessary to keep the church secure from fraud.

The church must also stay abreast of what is happening in its culture. It is often said that one of the best ways to learn lessons is from our mistakes. In most cases I agree heartily with this sentiment, but not here. When you are talking about fraud in the church, it is a lot less expensive to learn from someone else's mistakes. And in a church, the expense is not just lost money, it's often family members who are beloved leaders or employees that have difficult circumstances that make confronting them very difficult. Fraudulent activity takes a heavy toll emotionally and spiritually as well.

These days it is rather easy to find out what is going on. As part of its fraud awareness processes, the church anti-fraud team should perform Google© searches for church embezzlement and fraud. This simple step can provide a thorough education on what is happening to other churches. As long as this is done frequently, a church has a better chance of avoiding the headlines.

The anti-fraud team should also consult with professionals involved in fraud prevention. The churches external auditors can give valuable input and if specific problems are suspected, consulting with a Certified Fraud Examiner may also prove helpful. Also, local law enforcement officials can serve as another resource.

I repeat; fraudsters are hard at work looking for new ways to take your church's money. Make a commitment to stay one step ahead of them.

Weeds in the Garden

A Few Last Words

As we draw to a close I would like to leave you with a few last words. Not mine however. When I researched case stories to find illustrations, one of the things I focused on were words spoken by individuals involved in various church embezzlement situations. I have selected a few of my favorites, each of which makes an important point about the danger of fraud in the church house.

The classic reaction...

"She's been going to our church since 1999 and was a dear friend of ours…"
"She is someone that we loved and trusted; that we'd have over to our home for the holidays…. That's why we couldn't believe our own eyes when we started figuring out what happened…" [1]

These are some of the more famous fraud "last words." Seldom do gangsters come in and ransack or hold-up churches. Church embezzlements are usually the work of trusted, long-term employees. One of the hallmarks of "successful" thieves is their incredible ability to gain the confidence of their victims. Certified Fraud Examiners refer to this as "Social Engineering." A better way to put it is "playing a con-game."

A common theme... good people who have gotten themselves in trouble...

"Church officials reported that the pastor took church money because of a 'very powerful gambling addiction'.[2] *And in another situation, "church officials asked that their employee be spared prison as they believe she was stealing their money to pay for her husband's gambling debts."*[3]

These statements are representative of one of the most frequent causes of theft: good people find themselves in trouble and resort to "borrowing" from others to get their situation fixed. Fraud examiners refer to the "fraud triangle" which consists of pressure, opportunity, and rationalization. Gambling and other addictions, business setbacks, and health problems create economic pressures on church employees. When these pressures are combined with the ripe opportunity provided by far too many churches, rationalization becomes an easy proposition.

This church had no one to blame but itself!!!

"The pastor testified last week that church money he spent on trips to Las Vegas and rounds of golf was 'a small compensation' for his service." "His attorney said a loophole in the church's financial structure gave the pastor discretion to spend money." "He took advantage of that loophole, no question, but that loophole existed because the church allowed it, and that's not anyone's fault but the church, the pastor's attorney said in his closing arguments..."[4]

[2]The Associated Press. "Priest is Charged in Church Theft." New York Times 24 May 2008
[3]Katz, Nancie L. "No Jail in Deal for Church Embezzler." New York Daily News 11 April 2003
[4]The Associated Press. "Priest Found Guilty in Church Theft Trial." WPBF.com 23 February 2009

I find this quite bizarre; it is not the pastor's fault, it is the church's! I included this anecdote simply to remind us of the thinking that is prevalent in contemporary culture. This situation is good evidence that churches are not exempt or immune from the behavior that this type of thinking can spawn. But is a reminder that if discretionary funds are available, they must have accountability.

But the most important point of all...

"In 1999, Richard Kimsey and his wife, Susan, deposited $100,000 with a Phoenix-based Southern Baptist agency that promised to do the Lord's work. A few days later, the Kimseys' money had all but vanished…

"Money is not the issue," Susan Kimsey said. ***"This has been a black mark on Christianity as a whole."*** [5]

Church fraud prevention is not really about protecting cash and property. Even though the church's people are much more important than its bank accounts, the ultimate purpose is also not the protection of the employees and volunteers who handle the church's finances. The main function of fraud prevention in the church is protection of the Lord's name and the unimpeded furtherance of His work.

We should need no other reason to be serious about protecting our churches from the threat of fraud than holding the Lord's name high and furthering His kingdom's work.

[5]Sterling, Terry Greene. "Executives Sentenced in Church Fraud." The Washington Post 1 October 2006

Weeds in the Garden

Index

Additional Resources:

Weeds ın the Garden Workbook

This helpful companion to "Weeds in the Garden" is a download on the NACBA National web site. It provides a chapter by chapter workbook for congregational leaders to apply the principals and information found in the book. Code: M1324W

 **FACT!**

The PSK's **F**raud **A**wareness **C**hurch **T**est (FACT!) is a self-administered questionnaire and analysis process that lets you evaluate your church's risk and identify crucial areas of vulnerability. Organized around ten key concepts of effective fraud prevention, the process will guide you through about three hundred penetrating and enlightening questions. The report you will receive will give you a fresh look at areas where you may be at risk.

To participate go to **www.pskcpa.com**
and click on the FACT ! banner.

For additonal information and support contact:
www.pskcpa.com
1-800-424-5790

CPSIA information can be obtained at www.ICGtesting.com
Printed in the USA
LVOW082017060412

276488LV00001B/5/P